THE MAKING OF

GOLDENEYE

THE MAKING OF

GOLDENEYE

GARTH PEARCE

BOXTREE

Author and journalist Garth Pearce has interviewed film stars on location in thirty-two countries during the last twenty years. He is a former Showbusiness Editor of the *Daily Express* and his columns are now read in more than 100 leading publications around the world via the *New York Times* syndicate. *The Making of GoldenEye* is his sixth book.

First published in Great Britain in 1995 by Boxtree Limited

1 3 5 7 9 10 8 6 4 2

Designed by Martin Lovelock
Printed and bound in Italy

Boxtree Limited
Broadwall House · 21 Broadwall · London SE1 9PL

A CIP catalogue entry for this book is available from the British Library.

ISBN 1 85283 484 6

Picture Acknowledgements
Photographs were taken by:
Keith Hamshere: pp. 2, 6, 8, 8-9, 10 (bottom left), 11, 17, 18, 20, 21, 22, 22-23, 24 (top & bottom), 25 (top & bottom), 26-27, 28 (bottom right), 29, 30-31, 33, 34-35, 37, 38, 40, 42, 43, 44, 45, 46, 47, 49 (right), 51, 52, 53, 54-55, 57, 58-59, 60, 61, 62-63, 64, 65, 66, 67, 68, 69, 70-71, 72, 73, 74-75, 77, 78, 79, 81, 82, 83, 85, 86-87, 88, 89, 90, 92, 110, 110-11, 112-13, 114-15, 116, 117, 118, 119, 120, 121, 122-23, 125, 126

George Whitear: pp. 12, 13, 16, 19, 28 (top left), 39, 48, 49 (left), 50, 75 (bottom right), 91, 93, 94-95, 96, 98, 99, 100, 101, 102-103, 104, 105, 106-107, 107, 109, 115 (bottom right)

Terry O'Neill: pp.10 (top right), 95 (top right)

John Falkiner: pp.14-15, 108

Front cover photograph by Terry O'Neill
Back cover photograph by Keith Hamshere

Contents

Pierce Brosnan was in the driving seat from Day One on GOLDENEYE. He had to win the role all over again when the film was announced, and was determined to deliver.

JAMES BOND: PRESENT & CORRECT

James Bond has been impossible to kill. But there were those who had their doubts. A long-running legal battle over the future of 007 since he was last seen in the 1989 film *Licence to Kill* led some critics to think that perhaps Bond had shot the final bullet from his famous Walther PPK.

Producers Michael G. Wilson and Barbara Broccoli, thirty-five-year old daughter of Bond mastermind Cubby Broccoli, always had other ideas. In the face of cynics, they secretly began planning for *GoldenEye* early in 1993 with a commission to scriptwriter Michael France.

While France travelled to Moscow and St Petersburg to observe the current state of military intelligence in Russia, film giants MGM/UA gave their backing for what is the seventeenth Bond film.

When the script was delivered in April 1994, they all felt that here was a potential blockbuster. Bond would still be fighting his battles in Russia, but this time against a new order of mafia, gun-runners and the instant tycoons who have been created since the fall of Communism and the Berlin Wall.

Screenwriter France had interviewed KGB agents, toured military airfields and visited nuclear research laboratories in his efforts to present a setting of ruthless accuracy.

London-born writer Jeffrey Caine was invited to add his own ideas throughout the summer of 1994, with more revisions by Bruce Feirstein and Kevin Wade. Meanwhile Wilson, Broccoli and their company Eon Productions searched for locations and a studio base.

Ironically, Bond's most regular home at Pinewood Studios, Buckinghamshire and the giant 007 sound

Studio headquarters: The infamous Greenham Common, Berkshire was nearly chosen as the studio headquarters for *GoldenEye*. The American air base, the subject of long demonstrations by the 'Greenham Common Women' in the Eighties, was offered to Eon Productions. The site, abandoned shortly after the demolition of the Berlin Wall and end of the Cold War, has a two-mile runway which is 200 yards wide. But despite first-class facilities, including its own cinema, the Bond bosses decided that at sixty-five miles away it was just too far from London for a daily commute.

stage were unavailable because of a sudden increase in the number of British-made films. So apart from settling on locations in Russia, the Caribbean, the South of France, Switzerland and Monte Carlo, there was an unexpected and intense search for the right studio setting.

A former Rolls-Royce factory at Leavesden Airfield, near Watford, Hertfordshire, twenty miles from central

From Rolls-Royce, the mark of excellence, to James Bond, with the longest film series pedigree in the world. Work began on the conversion to a film studio six months before the first scene was shot.

London, came as a surprise choice. It was, until its closure in 1993, a working base for 3,000 men and women. Among its advantages was a disused runway, 1,000 yards long and fifty yards wide, which could be used for set-building and office space which could be converted to sound studios and administration headquarters.

Eon rented it on a contract of twelve months and two days from 28 June 1994 and began a rapid and massive conversion. Michael Wilson argued that financially it was not only going to be comparable to Pinewood, but had the added advantage of far more space and being exclusive to Bond actors and crew.

Amid the frantic re-organisation to bring Bond back to the screen, there came one important announcement. Actor Timothy Dalton, who had starred in both *Licence to Kill* and *The Living Daylights*, felt that six years was long enough to wait for his third appearance as 007, and wanted to call it a day.

The order went out: find a new James Bond.

The new James Bond: the key questions

Why Pierce Brosnan?

Debbie McWilliams, Casting Director, says: 'I considered ten actors – all British – because the role was completely re-assessed. Some of them will certainly become big stars in the next few years. No-one else came really close. Pierce is absolutely right for now. He has a great physical presence: extremely handsome and tall with a sexuality on screen. He can deliver humour, action and danger and there is a special air of mystery about him.'

Why the six-year delay from the last Bond film?

Producer Michael G. Wilson says: 'MGM/UA, the American film studio which financed and distributed Bond, was taken over. In order to make the whole thing work, the new owner was told that he could sell assets of the company. These assets included television and video rights to Bond films. Our company, Danjaq, owned by Mr and Mrs Broccoli, objected and there was a court injunction. This legal fight dragged on and on. Cubby Broccoli considered he was fighting for the film rights and authenticity of James Bond, past, present and future. It was finally settled at Christmas 1992, with MGM/UA under new ownership and Bond back on course to our satisfaction.'

Why go ahead with another Bond film, when there have been so many movie action heroes in recent years?

Director Martin Campbell says: 'Bond is unique. We are making an action adventure film, in exotic locations, with a superhero who has a panache and style like no other. It is a harder picture in terms of the action and much tougher. We have also made him a Bond for the Nineties. The new, female M calls him a sexist dinosaur. There are two major women's roles in this: a really bad girl and a woman who is more independent than any from Bond movies. But Bond can't help himself being a little sexist and he still has a great sense of humour.'

Left: The smile of success: the right man at the right moment.
Right: The great escape. Bond and Natalya (Izabella Scorupco) come to blows after ejecting themselves to safety seconds before their helicopter is hit by rockets.

Why Leavesden as a studio?

Peter Lamont, Production Designer, says: 'We looked at about four alternatives, but this had the perfect balance between office space and potential studio space on a site that was bigger than established studios like Pinewood and Shepperton. And it was only twenty miles from London. It was all ours, to develop and film as we liked, and we ended up with 1.25 million square feet of interior space and one of the biggest back lots in the world. The fact that it was originally opened in 1940 to manufacture the legendary Mosquito fighter bombers in the Second World War was also a nice touch.'

Why the choice of foreign locations?

Producer Barbara Broccoli says: 'Bond must always have glamour. Puerto Rico has the world's largest spherical radar-radio telescope, which becomes a fictional location in Cuba for our film, and it looks breathtaking. The real dish, at Arecibo, has produced maps of Venus and in 1974 beamed the Arecibo Message, describing life on Earth to anyone listening in outer space. We chose Monte Carlo because it is probably the glamour capital of the world, with casinos and a setting that Bond loves. St Petersburg in Russia is a stunning city. The authorities agreed to a tank chase in their streets, which proved irresistible.'

Left: Bond and CIA man Jack Wade drive his tiny Moskvich car through the faded elegance of St Petersburg, Russia.
Below: Sleek, expensive and fast. Bond's Aston Martin DB5 encounters Xenia's Ferrari 355.

GOLDENEYE: THE STORY

Pre-title sequence

James Bond is poised to plunge more than 600 feet alongside a wall of sheer concrete into a top secret Soviet nerve gas facility, carved out of solid rock below a huge dam in almost impenetrable mountain terrain.

As dawn breaks over the mountains, he jumps on a bungee cord, fires a piton gun into the concrete roof of the nerve gas plant and hauls himself slowly down the rest of the way.

On entry, he meets up with his 006 Secret Service colleague Alexander Trevelyan (Sean Bean). But their mission to blow up the plant is detected and Soviet hardman Colonel Ourumov (Gottfried John) leads a counter-attack.

Trevelyan is trapped. Bond has a choice: to abandon the operation and be captured or continue, leaving Trevelyan to try and fight his own way to freedom.

Being Bond, there is only one decision …

Instead of setting the timers on the explosive charges for six minutes, he sets them to go off in only three minutes' time. Bond makes his solo escape. In a struggle with the pilot of a plane which is taxiing to take off on the edge of a sheer drop, Bond and the pilot both fall to the ground, with the plane still gathering speed and no-one at the controls.

A soldier on a motorcycle, giving chase, swerves to avoid them and crashes. Bond picks himself up, jumps on to the riderless motorcycle and roars after the plane. Just as it disappears over the edge of the cliff, Bond does the unthinkable: he accelerates and sends himself – and the bike – hurtling after it, into the abyss.

Bond goes in to freefall, manoeuvering himself towards the plane. He grabs the wing-strut and hauls himself into the cockpit. With the ground hurtling towards him, he pulls out of the dive, just above the jagged rocks, as explosions rip apart the plant.

BOND IS BACK

Nine years later...

Bond drives his classic Aston Martin DB5 at speed along winding roads in the South of France, with its distinctive exhaust bellowing at the tight corners.

His passenger is Caroline (Serena Gordon), an immaculately-dressed young woman of impeccable background who has been sent by his new female boss M (Judi Dench) to evaluate him.

A Ferrari 355 pulls up alongside the DB5, with a beautiful woman, Xenia Onatopp (Famke Janssen) at the wheel. They conduct a high-speed game of cat-and-mouse, careering down the mountain road.

Bond finally allows the Ferrari to race ahead, as he pulls to the edge of the road with a view over Monte Carlo's shimmering sea. He thumbs open the top of the gear stick, presses a button and a small compartment slides forward. Inside: a chilled bottle of Bollinger champagne to share with Caroline.

That night Bond arrives at the casino in Monte Carlo, noticing the Ferrari parked by a valet near the door. Inside the casino he sees Xenia, looking stunning, she is playing baccarat and winning regularly.

Bond joins the table and beats her, with enormous

stakes. He introduces himself and reacts with some amusement when he learns that she is Russian and her name is Onatopp.

As he orders drinks, Admiral Chuck Farrell (Billy J. Mitchell) of the Canadian navy arrives to take her away.

Bond watches Xenia and the Admiral board a small launch with the name *Manticore* scripted across the stern. He views through a pair of night glasses, with a zoom camera lens, as the small boat reaches a sleek yacht of the same name, anchored in the harbour. Moored nearby is a French warship and on the stern the outline of a helicopter.

Miss Moneypenny (Samantha Bond) reports to 007 that the *Manticore* is leased to a known Janus Crime Syndicate in St Petersburg, Russia and Xenia Onatopp is an ex-Soviet fighter pilot. He should keep her under surveillance.

Xenia is locked in an intimate embrace with Admiral Farrell. She is on top, riding and pummelling him, coupling vigorously, almost violently. Farrell seems to be enjoying himself, but Xenia suddenly flips him over and wraps her muscular legs around his back.

She kisses him and squeezes powerfully in a scissor lock. He screams that he cannot breathe and she presses until there is a dull crack of bone.

The next day Bond watches as Xenia and the Admiral leave for the French warship. He enters the *Manticore*, which seems deserted. Despite a sudden attack by a crewman, he is able to discover the body of Admiral Farrell.

On realising that the 'Admiral' with Xenia is a decoy, he leaps on the boat's launch and heads for the warship. He is too late, despite a desperate dash, to stop Xenia and her partner stealing a valuable, top-secret NATO Tiger helicopter from the ship.

Xenia, at the controls, contemptuously loops the loop as she banks seaward out of sight.

A huge radio telescope dish is set against a bleak, snowy landscape and darkening sky of north Russia, just inside the Arctic Circle. It is a secret underground installation: Russia's Space Weapons Research Centre, called Severnaya.

In a bunker thirty feet below ground level, Natalya Simonova (Izabella Scorupco) works at her computer screen. In the adjacent console, the brilliant Boris Grishenko (Alan Cumming) is playing the computer keyboard with the energy and verve of a concert pianist.

It is late afternoon and Boris leaves momentarily for a cigarette, hunching himself against the cold air. As he does so, he sees the Tiger helicopter dropping from the sky and landing in a flurry of snow.

Xenia is accompanied by former Colonel Ourumov, the man who captured Trevelyan. He has since been promoted to General. He carries a metal briefcase. She carries a machine gun.

They move briskly down the stairs and Ourumov introduces himself to be allowed through the tight security. Natalya is brewing coffee in a small kitchen area, unaware of the VIP visit. The clock on the microwave oven shows the time at 16.09 (4.09pm).

Ourumov tells the duty officer that they are here to test-fire the secret space-based weapons programme, GoldenEye. Every scientist and technician watches as the GoldenEye – a disc to access codes – is handed over.

Xenia steps forward, unslings her machine pistol and shoots everyone in the room, apart from Ourumov, before the systematic turning of keys activates the system. Natalya listens and hides in horror. The badly wounded second officer punches an alarm button before being shot again.

At a Siberian airbase three pilots race on to the tarmac, where their MiG 29s are waiting, to respond to the alarm.

Ourumov takes the GoldenEye, slots it into the console, arms a weapon in space and sets the target at Severnaya itself. He puts the GoldenEye into his briefcase, snapping it shut.

In London, Bond meets Moneypenny at MI6 headquarters; she tells him that M (Judi Dench) wants him immediately to attend the situation room. The room is buzzing with activity, watching satellite pictures of Severnaya.

A senior analyst tells Bond that they have intercepted a distress call and are viewing as the Russians scramble three MiG 29s to the scene. They had also seen the stolen Tiger helicopter take off from Severnaya.

Natalya stares at her dead comrades, but sees from the screens that there is a countdown to an explosion. She flings herself further down a set of stairs as a nuclear charge explodes over Severnaya.

Two of the MiGs, flying one above the other, are enveloped in flashing coils of electrical charge; they collide and explode in a huge fireball. Blue flashes arc harmlessly around the Tiger's shielding, as it flies on unaffected. The third MiG, spinning out of control, disintegrates as it hits the ground.

Bond in thoughtful mood as he checks incoming satellite pictures with MI6 analyst Tanner (Michael Kitchen).

A massive steel structure, the centre point of the radio dish, crashes through the roof and Natalya suddenly has a means of escape. She searches, in vain, for Boris.

At MI6 headquarters, they report that their satellite, plus two American-owned, are knocked out. Another one eventually comes into range. Flickering pictures show a destroyed Severnaya and the crushed MiGs.

Bond observes that all electric lights in the nearby town have been wiped out. M reports that it is an Electro-Magnetic-Pulse: a nuclear device in the upper atmosphere to set up a radiation surge which destroys anything with an electronic circuit in a certain area.

Bond guesses that the mayhem could have been created to cover up the theft of the GoldenEye and notes from the screen that there is a heat image of someone still alive amid the wreck of Severnaya.

M asks Bond what he knows of the Janus syndicate. He tells her that they are top-flight arms dealers with headquarters in St Petersburg. Xenia Onatopp is the only confirmed contact. M says that having pulled files on anyone who might have had authority to access at Severnaya, General Ourumov is the top name on the list. He sees himself as the next Iron Man of Russia.

M orders Bond to find the GoldenEye, but not to avenge Trevelyan in the process of some personal vendetta with Ourumov.

Bond attends Q's workshop to be fitted out. A highly-refined BMW sports coupe car is one new addition, plus a leather belt with a 75-foot rappelling cord and an explosive pen.

In the council chamber of Winter Palace Square, St Petersburg, Defence Minister Dimitri Mishkin (Tcheky Karyo) listens to General Ourumov's report, claiming that the Severnaya destruction was by Siberian Separatists.

Mishkin asks about the two missing Severnaya

technicians – Boris and Natalya – and is told that there will be an investigation.

Bond arrives in St Petersburg on a direct British Airways flight to find CIA man Jack Wade (Joe Don Baker) ready to meet him, with a secret password. He tells him that his first contact in the investigation should be a tough ex-KGB man with a limp called Valentin Zukovsky (Robbie Coltrane). He's now part of the gun-running Mafia. Bond tells Wade that it was he who gave Valentin the limp.

After a long trek back to civilisation, Natalya reappears in a shopping arcade in St Petersburg. Entering a computer shop, she pretends to want to buy an IBM computer and tells the manager she has potential orders for thirty-five. He allows her to test them. She uses the opportunity to try and contact Boris on the Internet. They make contact, and he urges her to meet him at 6pm the following night.

Bond enters Valentin's lair and is almost immediately captured by five of his thugs. When Bond tells him he wants a favour, Valentin can hardly believe it, reminding 007 that he was virtually crippled by a shot from his Walther PPK.

Bond insists that he only shot his knee because he did not want to kill him. The two complete a verbal deal, based on Bond giving Valentin a chance to earn a fortune. In return, he wants a contact set up with Janus.

Valentin agrees to help, but says that he has never met him. All he knows is that he is a Lienz Cossack, a group who fought for the Nazis – against Russia – in the Second World War.

When the war ended the Lienz Cossacks surrendered to the British in Austria, expecting to join the government and go to war against communism. Instead, the British sent them back to Stalin, who promptly executed them.

Check-mate. Bond finds himself in an impossible situation, just when he thinks he has upstaged arms dealer Valentin (Robbie Coltrane).

Natalya makes her appointment with Boris. But he leads her purposely into the arms of Xenia, who immediately stuns her with one blow.

In his hotel swimming pool, Bond eases the tensions of the day with a succession of fast turns. On getting out, he walks to the steam room where Xenia awaits. She pretends to be attracted to him, circling her arms around his wet body. But within seconds, she has wrapped her legs around him and is squeezing the life from his lungs.

But Bond fights back, grabbing his gun, and orders Xenia to take him to Janus.

Xenia guides him by car to a statue park. This is not a public park, but a section of the municipal dump reserved for political refuse: the unwanted statues of Lenin, Marx, Stalin and others, in granite, bronze, steel and plaster.

Bond delivers a short, sharp rabbit punch on the back of Xenia's neck, takes the car keys and climbs out.

Alec Trevelyan, 006, steps into the light, apparently back from the dead. His face has changed, with the right

Bond feels the first potentially fatal squeeze from Xenia (Famke Janssen), during her attempt to seduce him in a St Petersburg spa.

side marked by a clumsy skin graft.

Bond stands, staring in stunned silence. His steely cool has deserted him.

When he recovers from the shock, Bond asks how MI6 screening missed the fact that Trevelyan was a Lienz Cossack. He replies that his parents escaped Stalin's execution squads, but committed suicide in shame. The British government had figured Trevelyan was too young to remember.

A stun dart fired into his neck knocks Bond off his feet. He slumps, unconscious.

Bond comes around to discover he is bound in the front seat of the stolen Tiger helicopter. There is a frantic pounding from behind his seat, where he discovers Natalya, strapped in, kicking.

Two missiles jet off, screaming low and arcing up and away. Bond watches the rockets, confounded, as they loop back and target the Tiger.

He slams his head on the seat ejector button and both

he and Natalya are launched in the cabin capsule as the rockets scream in to the helicopter and explode.

The capsule tumbles in flight, a parachute opening, breaking the free fall, but still landing with a violent thud as it is so close to the ground.

Jeeps roar in and both Bond and Natalya are taken by soldiers to a basement interrogation room at military intelligence headquarters.

Bond notices that Natalya's watch has stopped at the very time Severnaya was blasted. He deduces that she is the person who escaped. Natalya tells him of the slaughter, and that the inside traitor was Boris.

Defence Minister Mishkin (Tcheky Karyo) personally conducts the interrogation that follows, with Bond's gun on his desk. Natalya reveals that she saw General Ourumov set off the explosion and steal GoldenEye.

Within seconds, Ourumov enters, kills Mishkin and a guard with Bond's Walther PPK, empties the

magazine, then throws the useless gun to 007.

He yells to guards outside that Bond has killed Mishkin. Before they can react, Bond fells two of them, scoops up their discarded machine pistol, grabs Natalya and runs into the corridor.

A fierce fight follows in the cavernous file room of Military Intelligence Archives. Natalya falls through the shattered floor into the grip of Ourumov and guards.

Bond pulls off his belt, aims the buckle at the ceiling and fires, as instructed by Q. The fine tensile wire shoots out, the piton embeds itself and he swings like Errol Flynn towards a circular window and drops in to the tarpaulin canopy of a lorry.

Bond watches Ourumov leave the building in a car with Natalya captive. He turns and sees a row of tanks. He struggles with the unfamiliar controls of one of them and gives chase.

A sensational tank chase follows, with bridge, road island and alley way being destroyed. A Perrier lorry is sliced in half, spraying hundreds of cans into the air. The tank then plunges in to a statue of Tsar Nicholas, sitting astride a winged horse, destroying the plinth and leaving the statue perched on the tank's turret.

Ourumov manages to get his car to the railway station, forcing Natalya to board the Janus command centre, a train with a huge armour-plated battering ram built on to the front of a powerful diesel engine.

As the train pulls away, she is brought to Trevelyan's dining carriage, with Xenia in attendance. The train is heading towards open country when the tank looms out of the darkness of the tunnel, on the rails.

Trevelyan orders the engineer to go full speed ahead and ram the tank. Bond fires the tank's huge gun and the train's engine explodes. The burnt-out wreck of the engine, still dragging the carriage along, collides with the tank.

Bond enters Trevelyan's dining carriage, gun at the ready. All those inside are stunned and hurt – but alive. Ourumov still has Natalya in his grip and is threatening to kill her.

Bond shoots him dead with a single shot, but turns to

confront Trevelyan … too late. Automatic locks and shutters slam into place, leaving just Bond and Natalya in the carriage.

Trevelyan, with Xenia at his side, aims a remote control at an ominous-looking freight car still sticking out of the tunnel; the freight car sides drop away, revealing a sleek black helicopter.

Natalya sees a computer screen and suspects that, somewhere, Boris is on-line, backing up his files. As she begins to trace his whereabouts Bond is warned by Trevelyan on a speaker that explosive timers have been set in the carriage for six minutes: 'The same six minutes as you gave me,' he says, as he flies away with Xenia.

Bond realises that he only has three minutes to save them both. He uses the thin laser beam of his watch to cut open the floor.

Natalya is able to trace Boris's whereabouts to Northwest Cuba. Bond pulls her from the seat and they both drop through the hole in the floor seconds before the explosion.

On a dusty Caribbean island road in the twilight, only one vehicle is moving, an open-top BMW sports car.

Bond is at the wheel, Natalya, looking radiant, is sitting next to him.

There is a bleep from the car and Bond looks down at the radar screen. Moments later, a light plane comes into view, landing in front of them on the road.

It is Jack Wade. He gives a small case to Bond, containing satellite maps. They are looking for a dish the size of a football field, and he offers little hope.

They swap vehicles: Wade takes the BMW, Bond and Natalya the plane: 'Cuba is eighty miles on your right,' the CIA man says.

By the time they have circled Cuba, they are prepared to believe Jack Wade. There is no sign of any dish – only a peaceful lake. As they circle once more, a missile erupts out of the water, hitting the plane's wing.

They plunge towards the lake, aquaplane on to the shore and towards the dense trees of a jungle. After the impact, Bond and Natalya slump exhausted.

A helicopter, silhouetted against the sun, hovers above the clearing. From its underbelly hangs a long rope on which a dark figure is abseiling down towards Bond.

Bond staggers to his feet, only to be smashed to the ground by the boot of the abseiling figure: it's Xenia,

prepared to kill. Again, she puts him between her thighs, which have the strength of a boa constrictor.

An exhausted Bond reaches and grabs a machine pistol strapped to her back and fires wildly towards the hovering helicopter. The panicked pilot pushes the helicopter forward as bullets hit the undercarriage.

The rope tightens around Xenia, violently jerking her backwards off her feet against the forked limbs of a tree, breaking her back and neck. The helicopter tips sideways and plunges into the jungle, with Xenia's body still hanging in the tree.

Boris is operating a vast triple-level underground command and control centre, with giant screens dominating the lower level. Trevelyan urges him on. Their aim: to break into world banks by computer and transfer money electronically seconds before GoldenEye is set off to erase any record of transactions.

It will cause a financial melt-down around the world. Outside, Bond and Natalya discover that the lake they saw was nothing more than a cover for three telescopic masts joined by steel cables. The lake recedes and the shape of a huge dish, hundreds of feet in diameter, emerges. It is a giant radio dish.

They see that on the vast superstructure, 500 feet up, the cradle is rotating. Natalya says that Trevelyan must be set to signal a satellite for another explosion. The only way to stop it is to get to the transmitter, above the antenna.

Five men with automatic weapons start shooting at them. They slide together down the slimy surface of the dish to the centre and climb into a hatch.

This starts the final countdown to a spectacular hand-to-hand fight to the finish between Bond and Trevelyan as 007 attempts to destroy the control centre and the threat to world peace and stability.

PIERCE BROSNAN'S BOND DIARY

Pierce Brosnan took the telephone call at exactly 12.35pm on 1 June 1994 at his home in Malibu, California: 'Hello, Mr Bond,' said his agent, Fred Spector. 'You've got the part.'

They were the words Brosnan had longed to hear. But he remained calm: no victory cheer, no wild celebration. James Bond had already played such an important role in his own life, mixed with soaring excitement, bitter disappointment and even tragedy that he could afford to control his emotions.

Instead, he returned to the swimming pool of his spectacular house – with its six acres of land and views from terraces and balconies over the Pacific Ocean it could be a setting for a scene from any 007 film – to sit quietly and reflect.

Brosnan thought back to another telephone call from his agent in this same home on a Thursday afternoon in July 1986, which spelled the end of a disturbing sequence of events.

He had then turned to his wife, actress Cassandra Harris, to tell her: 'James Bond is finished for me. Over. I am never going to get it now.'

Pierce remembered her own disappointment: how she seemed numbed at the empty prospect. Cassie had appeared opposite Roger Moore in *For Your Eyes Only* in 1980, when Pierce had merely been a visitor on the set. It had always been a kind of in-joke between them: 'One day,' said Cassie, 'you'll be Bond.'

As Brosnan's own career progressed, with a move to Hollywood, a successful TV series, *Remington Steele* and the movie, *The Fourth Protocol*, his name suddenly was being talked about as the next 007 to succeed Roger Moore.

In a flurry of meetings and screen tests in the summer of 1986, with *Remington Steele* officially at an end, he was offered and accepted the role. But, in the background, there was a catch which would put a stop to his plans. *Remington Steele* makers, MTM Television, had a clause in his contract that they had sixty days to try and re-sell the show.

With the sudden surge of publicity for his James Bond role, with costume fittings going ahead and initial locations already earmarked for Gibraltar and Austria, MTM began to get interested once again in *Remington Steele*.

They were able to sell a new series of the show to NBC Television, on the strength of Pierce being the new Bond. He would have to film six more episodes. But with cruelty of timing, it happened to be on the sixtieth and final afternoon of his contract pick-up.

'Actors lose very big roles every week which they have fought for and deserve, but never one so publicly,' recalls Pierce. 'There was absolutely nothing I could do. It was out of my control.

'My relationship with Cassie was very strong, in that we fought all our battles together. But on this one, she took it more on the chin than I did. She was heartbroken.

'It was me who was calming her. I was saying it did not matter and we had to move on. We had done our best. Someone out there did not want me to do it. In truth, I felt numb. But I was so concerned about her that the words somehow came.

'I then went out and played a lot of tennis. That is how I got out some of the anger and aggression. For a while, I thought that perhaps it had not affected me too much. But I must have been kidding myself.'

Six months passed. English actor Timothy Dalton, a late choice, had settled into filming. Reports from Gibraltar and Vienna, Austria, were good. He was an action man who took the role deadly seriously.

'I know Tim, he's a nice guy and I wished him well,' says Pierce. 'But one afternoon I was driving along Pacific Coast Highway, a few miles from my home, and it all started going around in my head what could have been and what I should have been doing.

'I became so angry that I had to stop the car. I ranted and raved and shouted to myself along a quiet stretch of the road, with just the sound of the gulls and the sea. I thought to myself: "You have lost it, Brosnan. This is it. Don't let them get to you. Just get back in the car and drive on."

'Eventually, I did. Very slowly. That is when I came to terms with the fact that not getting Bond was never going to leave me. However spectacular my career might be, I'd still be known for that. It was a deeply depressing thought, yet I was going to have to come to terms with it over the coming years.'

Timothy Dalton was to make two Bond films, *The Living Daylights* and *Licence to Kill*, before Danjaq, the parent company of Eon Productions, makers of Bond movies, became locked in a legal battle which dragged on and on.

Pierce, meanwhile, was dealing with far more serious problems. Cassie, whom he had met in 1978 and married two years later, was told at Christmas 1987, that she had terminal ovarian cancer. He put his acting career on hold, despite her urging him to carry on.

In the following four years, before Cassie's tragic death on 28 December 1991, aged thirty-nine, Pierce appeared in just two films: *The Lawnmower Man* and *Mister Johnson*. For a year after Cassie's death, which came with awful timing on the day after their eleventh wedding anniversary, Pierce was in mourning.

He did little and travelled and worked rarely. It somehow put his love affair with Bond into some perspective. But even late in 1993, after an hilarious performance opposite Robin Williams in the international hit, *Mrs Doubtfire*, he was telling me in New York: 'James Bond refuses to go away. I am going to be beaten with that one until I do something of real significance on screen'.

On 12 April 1994 with at last a firm prospect for a

006 and 007 all set for action. Bond, with friend and colleague Alec Trevelyan (Sean Bean), infiltrates a top-secret nerve gas plant.

new 007 film, Timothy Dalton announced that he thought it should no longer be him in the leading role. He telephoned the author from Charleston, South Carolina, where he was filming a TV mini-series, *Scarlett*, based on the long-awaited follow-up story of *Gone With The Wind*, to say: 'This has been one of the hardest decisions of my life.

'But it has been six years since the last Bond film and if I committed to the new one, it would be another two years of my life, what with filming and promotion. I think the time is right for me to say goodbye to it all.'

The race was on for a new Bond. Brosnan reluctantly began to think: could it be me? He was now forty-one. It was his last chance. Part of him still desperately wanted the role that had meant so much to

both him and Cassie; another more pragmatic emotion was there, however. Who, after all, had ever competed for and won a highly-desirable movie role, twice over?

Other actors' names were mentioned. Mel Gibson had allegedly been offered $15 million. Hugh Grant, suddenly the new British star in the wake of *Four Weddings and a Funeral*, was a contender. Others,

Pure Gold: Pierce Brosnan's very first visit to the cinema, aged eleven, was to see *Goldfinger* at the Odeon in Putney High Street, London in the summer of 1964: 'I remember seeing Shirley Eaton's gorgeous body painted in gold and thought: 'Wow … I wish I was James Bond.'

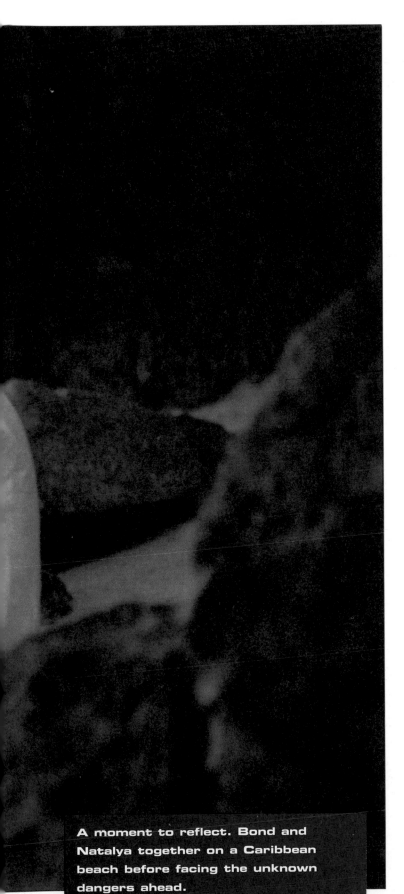

A moment to reflect. Bond and Natalya together on a Caribbean beach before facing the unknown dangers ahead.

including Liam Neeson, were touted in magazines.

They were inaccurate reports, but Brosnan could have found it unsettling. Instead he ignored them. 'I did not seek Bond this time. The moment Timothy jumped ship, I thought: "No. It won't happen a second time."

'Friends would send notes saying I had been nominated by this poll or that poll as the most suitable Bond. I just did not let it get to me. The last time had been such an unpleasant experience, I did not want to dare hope in case the whole thing crashed down around my ears again.'

Meetings had been held in secret with Bond mastermind, producer Cubby Broccoli, his stepson Michael G. Wilson and his daughter Barbara, who at thirty-four was finally making her producing debut with *GoldenEye*.

Because Pierce knew that the chances of winning the same part twice in a lifetime were slim, when he took the telephone call on that clear blue June afternoon he remained controlled. There had been so much personal history connected with the role, he wanted to savour it rather than shout and scream with triumph.

It was as if the famous Bond film title, *You Only Live Twice*, had returned to bless him and he still could not quite believe it.

Brosnan was joined by girlfriend Keely Shaye-Smith, an American broadcaster and former model, whom he had begun dating a month before. Then son Sean, eleven, returned home from school and the telephone calls began.

Daughter Charlotte, twenty-two, was in New York; son Christopher, twenty-one, was in London. Both were from Cassie's relationship with Dermot Harris, but were adopted by Pierce in 1980, and it is he whom they call Dad. He began to sense the first surge of heady excitement.

Pierce's mother May, a retired nurse in Wimbledon, London, rang him from 6,000 miles away to offer her own special congratulations.

Says Pierce: 'Life then went into full throttle. But I really had no idea of what was to come.'

8 June 1994

The luxuriously-appointed Regent Hotel in London, was opened in 1899 as The Grand Central. The idea behind the magnificent building might have appealed to James Bond writer, Ian Fleming. It was designed by Sir Edward Watkins with the prospect of the channel tunnel from France terminating at Marylebone railway station, just behind the hotel.

Although his vision never came to reality, even a century later it seemed the perfect place to launch a new James Bond. After nearly four years of hotel renovation, an eight-storey crystal palace of Winter Garden and gigantic palm trees gave an atmosphere of fantasy.

Pierce Brosnan was nervous. He was on his way from Los Angeles to Papua New Guinea, to film the lead role of Robinson Crusoe in a new film to which he had committed before Bond. This was the only day to launch his name and face properly to the world's TV stations, radio and newspapers.

He arrived, to be immediately flanked by two bodyguards. But Brosnan was surprised to discover that Bond co-producer Barbara Broccoli was even more nervous than he was: 'I then realised that she had not done one of these things before, either. Although she has worked on Bond films for years, her father Cubby had only handed over fully since the last film, so we were all new to it. I thought: "Stay cool. Think of this as a celebration." '

In the vast ground floor drawing room, there were nearly 300 media people including more than twenty-five key television crews. Geoff Freeman, unit publicist and a friend of Pierce since they worked together in 1986 on *The Fourth Protocol*, asked: 'Are you okay?'

Says Pierce: 'I was standing behind a screen and on the other side were the press of the world, waiting. I could hear the James Bond theme music had started. I was certainly aware enough to know that once I stepped from behind that screen, my life was going to change for ever.

'But nothing could quite prepare me for the pandemonium once I went through. The glare of the lights, cameramen yelling 'Pierce, Pierce, Pierce …' It's like everyone wants a piece of you. All I could do was smile and try to be gracious.

'I still didn't know how I was going to play Bond. I said that he's a killer. He has to have a sense of humour. He likes women. But we have to let the audience into his life.

'I had grown a beard in anticipation of doing Crusoe, so I didn't actually feel much like Bond. I answered the questions as best as I could and interviews were non-stop throughout the day. The last one I did was with a big skinny guy from Chicago and he was such a smart bastard. I did think to myself: "Oh, Christ." '

Three hours of talking followed, with a press conference, group interviews, recorded TV interviews and two live satellite links to America. Brosnan finally returned alone to the low-key Draycott Hotel in Cadogan Gardens, where the only outward sign that it is a hotel at all is a small brass plate.

'I lay on the bed in my suite and thought: "What the hell have I said 'Yes' to? What have I got myself involved in? Oh, God, Cassie. Cassie! Are you up there? Can you hear? Am I supposed to feel this shitty? I felt like the life had been sucked out of me." '

After a restless night, he walked to an early breakfast at Chelsea Kitchen along the King's Road, a place he used to visit with his late wife. It was quiet and he was

Son of Bond: Pierce Brosnan regularly has his hands 'doubled' by son Christopher, now twenty-two. The first is pulling on a hand-brake in a car chase scene in the Aston Martin DB5. Then he flips open the glove compartment to reveal a bottle of chilled Bollinger champagne. Christopher, a third assistant trainee on the second unit, is again in action when a close-up of Bond's hand is needed using a laser in the opening bungee jump sequence and cutting through the floor of a train.

able to read the British morning newspapers, undisturbed, to find that his role of James Bond had become headline news in every one of them.

Exactly twenty-four hours later, Brosnan was walking through undergrowth near a village in Papua New Guinea, between the first scenes of Crusoe. There was work to do and he had tried to block off his role as 007. He would think about that later.

Suddenly, a group of children were pointing excitedly at him: 'James Bond! James Bond!' Pierce stopped and turned to them: 'What did you say?'

'James Bond! James Bond!' they shouted.

'I was dumbstruck,' says Pierce. 'Here was I, in the middle of nowhere, being recognised as Bond as a result of all that international publicity. At that moment any lingering doubts I had that *GoldenEye* was just another film left me completely.'

16 January 1995

Just three miles from the M25, the driver's nightmare which circles London, is Leavesden Airfield, a former Rolls-Royce factory near Watford, Hertfordshire where Mosquito planes were built during the Second World War.

This morning, Pierce Brosnan was joining the slow-moving traffic for the first time in a chauffeur-driven Mercedes from his elegant Georgian five-bedroom rented house in Hampstead, London.

It is the most unusual setting in Bond's thirty-three-year film history. The sprawling factory site, deserted like a ghost town for the previous eighteen months, has been converted to a film studio with six sound stages, lavish dressing rooms, special effects and model-making areas, carpenter and plasterer shops and a viewing theatre.

But as Brosnan's car edged underneath the red and white barrier at the security gate, the signs of a desolate factory campus were still very much in evidence. A line of rusty bike sheds, with blue corrugated roof; a faded 20 miles an hour speed limit warning; a pedestrian crossing, with broken beacon; a ramshackle building

Despite the injury to his hand, Pierce Brosnan manages a dramatic escape from the Russian archive.

with a sign which says BP Lubricants; black windows staring down from disused offices, with brown scrubland grass poking defiantly from cracked concrete.

'From this setting, we have to create some magic,' says Pierce. 'All I am thinking on this first day is that I don't want to mess it up. The stakes are high, the expectations are high and it is important to get it right from the very first moment.'

Brosnan had been unsettled by a one-week delay to filming, caused by an accident to his hand. At this point, he could not even hold a gun properly and was having daily physiotherapy to get it right.

Before Christmas, he had a small operation on his

Appearing as Russian arms dealer Valentin Zukovsky, Robbie Coltrane keeps a straight face on screen.

back, which was causing problems. He wanted to be fitter than he'd ever been for Bond and had possibly been over-stretching himself.

There were many stories on how he had injured his hand, all pandering to the manly James Bond action-man image. One was that he had damaged fingers hang-gliding; another that he was repairing a corral on his ranch. In truth, he had been gingerly lifting himself up in his bathroom at home in Malibu, using a porcelain towel-rail as support. It snapped, severing tendons in his fingers, leading to treatment at hospital.

When Pierce told fellow actors and crew of what happened, nothing acted as a faster ice-breaker; they warmed instantly to his vulnerability and honesty.

'I feel such a prat making that one public,' he said, disarmingly. 'On the way to hospital I was thinking: "I don't believe it. So close to the role of a lifetime – and now this!" But I'm not treating it as a bad omen.'

His first day is a big scene: five pages of dialogue and action with twenty-two stone Robbie Coltrane, who is playing the Russian gun dealer Valentin. The two actors have not met socially since a charity event last year. But instantly the comical side of Coltrane bursts into action.

'Pierce makes a great Bond and he's the very best choice,' he says. 'He is ridiculously handsome. He also has a nice sense of humour. On top of that, he's a great fella. And he's talented. My God, I hate him already! You hold him down and I'll kick the hell out of him.'

Pierce, dressed in a grey suit after an hour spent in hair and make-up, has his own method of dealing with first day nerves: 'I'm thinking: "Keep it simple," ' he says. And, looking at Coltrane, he adds: 'I keep on saying to myself: "Don't take your eyes off him." '

By the end of the day, Bond is holding a gun to Valentin's head, with the hammer pulled back: 'Walther PPK, 7.65 mm,' observes Valentin, without looking around. 'Only three men I know use that gun – and I have killed two of them.'

'Lucky me,' says Bond.

22 January 1995

The skies are layered slate grey, the rain falls steadily and the car parks around the main sound stages at Leavesden are full of vehicles owned by camera crews and journalists. After the first of what will be twenty weeks of six-day working, twelve hours a day, Pierce Brosnan is ready to launch himself to the world at what has become his workplace.

The song, 'Nobody Does It Better', which has become like an unofficial anthem of 007, blasts from loudspeakers as a total of 400 journalists and forty camera crews, including two which have flown in from Peru and Japan to be here, wait for the introduction of the cast.

Ready to ride: Pierce Brosnan and Sean Bean face the TV cameras and press, using the legendary Aston Martin DB5 as their backdrop.

Pierce is introduced on the podium by Eon's Director of Marketing, Gordon Arnell and in turn calls in the rest of the cast, one by one. Sean Bean (Trevelyan) says he is off later to carry on filming his own movie, *When Saturday Comes*, and has been transported by helicopter from the set for a fleeting visit. It can only happen on Bond.

Robbie Coltrane, as ever, jokes: 'At the age of forty-four and this weight, I thought my chance of being a Bond girl was slim. And I must say, Pierce is an absolute gentleman in the shower scene.'

Signs that the cast is truly international are delivered from the tall, angular Famke Janssen (Xenia) who gives a short speech in both her native Dutch and English. Not to be outdone, Izabella Scorupco (Natalya) speaks in Swedish (she lives in Sweden), Polish (she was born in Poland) and English.

Samantha Bond (Moneypenny) says spiritedly: 'I have had jokes about my name all my life and it's great to be standing next to the real Bond.'

Then come the photographs, with Pierce surrounded, perched on the edge of an Aston Martin DB5. A BMW, to be used later in the film and only officially launched at the time of *GoldenEye*, is said to be in a large wooden crate marked 'Top Secret.' In reality the case is empty, but there's a guard dog in attendance, just in case any photographer becomes too ambitious.

Brosnan eventually sits underneath an old poster of Bond, screaming: GOLDFINGER – JAMES BOND IS BACK,' with a memorable photograph of Shirley Eaton's gold-painted body, eyes closed, stretched out. Ironically, Goldfinger was Brosnan's first introduction to Bond, in a London cinema in 1964, aged eleven, shortly after his move to Wimbledon from Ireland with his mother.

This time, TV crews and radio journalists include

Friendship long over, the action gets serious. Trevelyan tries to eliminate his former colleague in the Cuban control centre.

those from Bond's old enemy of Eastern Europe: Poland, Hungary, The Czech Republic, plus the TASS News Agency from Russia.

There are questions that Pierce expects, on the Bond girls: 'These are leading actresses in their own right,' he answers. 'We will call them leading ladies. But Izabella has luscious lips and Famke has great legs.' And questions that he does not: 'No, I didn't call my own son Sean after Sean Connery. I've honestly never thought about that one before.'

On the role, he answers: 'We have done one week's filming and I am still trying to find my way to the dressing room and discover all the corners of this lofty set of buildings.

'I am working with a lot of people who have done many Bond films before. But however supportive and embracing they are, I am going to be judged against my predecessors. The shoes of Roger Moore and Sean Connery are very big shoes to fill.'

7 February 1995

Dame Judi Dench has hardly slept at all. She is more than nervous. Petrified comes close, she says. For an actress who has delivered two or three hours of Shakespeare on stage, night after night, her three days and a few lines as the first female M on Bond have become like a mountain to climb.

She arrives on set, holding hands with her twenty-two-year-old actress daughter, Finty Williams: 'I will feel deeply depressed and will probably cry tomorrow,' she tells an amazed Brosnan. 'I will think of all the ways I *could* have done this.'

Pierce admits that he's terrified of her — and that's true, since he had discussed it for several days beforehand — and points out that her superb track record leaves him feeling vulnerable. How on earth could she be nervous of films when she can hold her own so brilliantly on stage?

But she says: 'I am slow to the boil and in theatre I find I can improve each performance. However well or badly you do it, there is always the next night and a chance to get it right or improve.

'With this, it's got to be right very quickly indeed. I can also feel the mood of a theatre audience, but I never know with a camera. I have also never watched myself on film. That's true. Never.'

It's all an ice-breaker. Not for the first time, Pierce finds himself in the role of comforter before going out to deliver what is an intense scene for the camera.

Judi is dressed to unsettle the chauvinistic Bond: a suit of creme heavy crepe, brown sheer tights, grey hair closely cropped, distinctive blue eyes made up to appear particularly steely.

Despite nerves, she delivers a crisp, cynical verbal attack on Bond, starting: 'I think you're a sexist, misogynist dinosaur … A relic of the cold war.'

But it's a long speech and there is a stumble: 'I'm sorry,' she says. 'I buggered that up.'

Pierce, for his part, makes a mistake on the next take, with the line: 'I have never forgotten that a licence to kill is also a certificate to die.' He says 'licence to die' instead.

'Well, that's one each,' observes director Martin Campbell, aware that it's a tricky scene, with the use of telephones, pop-up screens and computer gimmicks.

Campbell has already agreed that Judi does not light a cigarette during the scene. Her hand is shaking so much, it just doesn't work. She's also a non-smoker and fears choking mid-sentence.

A drink, though, does have to be served. Her offer to Bond is taken as reference to cognac which the old M used to pour so readily: 'I prefer bourbon,' she says. 'Ice?'

Two good measures of whisky are poured from a decanter. In reality, it's apple juice inside — and the ice consists of two lumps of light glass.

Says Pierce: 'Working opposite Dame Judi is going to be one of the highlights of this film. The moment I knew she had been cast, it was always going to be a special few days. It was reassuring to know that she's just as nervous.'

10 February 1995

Desmond Llewelyn arrives to play Q in a crumpled green suit, announcing that he has worn it non-stop for the last two weeks to give it an uncared for appearance. Desmond, who admits to seventy-six, is a warm and gloriously eccentric figure.

'I am hopeless with gadgets,' he tells an amused Pierce Brosnan. 'I can't even get a ticket to work in one of those confounded machines on the London Underground. And I can hardly put on a kettle, let alone set a video.'

Desmond has now appeared in every one of the Bond movies since the second, *From Russia With Love* in 1963, apart from Roger Moore's first, *Live And Let Die*, in which he was talked about but never seen.

'I am unique in the film business because I am a small-part actor who is known around the world for this one part,' says Desmond. 'My fame completely out-matches the reality.

'I get people saying to me: "Can you remember the line you said in so-and-so?" And then they quote it to me, word perfect. Remember it? I can't even remember the line I have to say today!'

The film crew is prepared, and well-used to his notorious lack of memory. On Bond's entrance to Q's workshop, Desmond has to sit in a wheelchair, with one leg extended in a full cast.

'Sorry about your leg, Q,' observes Bond. 'Skiing?'

Suddenly the foot of the cast drops open and a rocket fires across the workshop and through a leaded curtain, exploding into the far wall.

'Hunting,' says Q.

He then has to slip off the cast, stand up, lead Bond across the room, and point to a brand new BMW sports coupé being fitted by several men.

Desmond's next few lines are written large on a white wall behind the car: 'Now pay attention 007. First, your new car. BMW. Agile. Highly refined. Six forward gears, all-points radar, self-destruct system,

'Now pay attention, 007.' Q's brief on the advantages of the new BMW, with its own very special 'optional extras'.

stinger missiles behind the headlamps.'

On Take One, the lights are shining at a harsh angle and Desmond loses sight of the words. He gets to 'self-destruct' and stops. Seconds later, too late, his eyes pick up the word 'system'. Cut.

The writing on the wall is replaced by four separate cue cards – 'Q cards' joke the crew – held by assistants.

Take Two. 'First, your new car …' Desmond fails to find where the second assistant is standing for the next line. Cut.

Take Three. He can't quite get out of the wheelchair and stumbles. 'Damn,' he says. Cut.

Take Four. As he gets out of the wheelchair, his hand accidentally knocks on the four flashing warning lights. He completes the scene, word perfect, but it's all unusable because of a winking orange glow.

The film crew have huge smiles on their faces as director Martin Campbell jokes: 'I am wondering about an ejector wheelchair. Desmond just lands in the BMW with a list of instructions.'

It's all light relief and Desmond laughs with the rest: 'Roger Moore was a great practical joker and knew of my tendency to forget lines,' he recalls. 'Just before going on one day, he presented me with a whole new page of script, full of technical detail. I nearly dropped dead!'

Says Pierce: 'I feel as if I am a different character in a different film today – like a John Cleese farce.'

13 February 1995

There are beautiful girls everywhere. They arrived at dawn and are now dressed in backless and sleeveless dresses of gold, blue, red, green and black warmed by heaters on the vast A stage.

It is the casino scene and set-builders have provided white wooden walls, oil paintings, Roman-like motifs, roulette wheels and blackjack tables, plus what looks like a fully-stocked long bar.

'This is what Bond is all about,' says Pierce, as he peers at the scene. 'Glamour!'

Christina Pile gets the chance to put her theories to the test on GOLDENEYE. The dress designer, who did a thesis on Bond Girls for her degree, provided seven dresses for the casino scene. This is one of them.

He's in a dichotomy. On the one hand, he realises a vital ingredient of all 007 movies is stunning girls. On the other, he has decided not to be photographed in a group or pyramid shot with any of them. He feels that Bond, in his first film in the 1990s, should move on from that straight 'glamour picture' image.

Also, this is the day he delivers the two famous James Bond catchphrases, which have passed into movie folklore: 'The name is Bond, James Bond.' And: 'Vodka Martini, shaken not stirred.'

He says: 'I am okay with the Vodka Martini, because it's a drink I like and I genuinely order them. One of those sets you up for the night. Four of them and you're anybody's.

'But saying "Bond, James Bond" is another matter. I was there cleaning my teeth this morning saying it over and over again. I felt very foolish with toothpaste running all over my chin.

'I have refused to say it in public or rehearsals, because it's a line you can deliver in so many different ways. And I could trip up over it and I can imagine a situation where we're on the tenth take and my hands are starting to sweat.'

One of the girls in the casino scene is twenty-six year-old actress Kate Gayson, whose mother Eunice appeared at the gambling tables opposite Sean Connery in his *Dr No* debut.

'My mother said that those first lines of "Bond, James Bond" took thirty-two takes, because Sean was trembling with nerves,' she tells Pierce. 'He kept on giving his own name, "Sean, Sean Bond". And then there was "James, James Connery". In the end, he'd lost it completely.

'My mom was told to take him out and give him a couple of whiskies. She gave him a good tot of scotch and that eased his tension, so he delivered it in the first take after lunch.'

Pierce listens, his own tension visibly easing: 'That makes me feel a lot better,' he smiles.

The girls for the scene have been hired from a variety of sources, mostly model agencies. They include nineteen-year-old Rachel Parsons, a Julia Roberts look-alike from Essex; Paula Marriott, thirty-four, a graphic designer from Maidenhead, Berkshire (whose son played Prince William in the American TV film *Diana – Her True Story*) and German actress Simone Bechtel, twenty-eight, who won a competition organised by giant film distributors UIP to have a walk-on part in a Bond film.

There's also dress designer Christina Pile, who did a thesis on Bond Girls at Nottingham University and has now been given a chance to put her theories to the test, delivering a set of seven dresses at up to £1,000 each for the glamorous scene.

'As part of my thesis, I watched videos of all sixteen Bond films in the last thirty-two years, freeze-framed them on every girl and took photographs of each dress,' she says. 'Whatever the fashion of the time, the secret is

Bond, always playing to win, is ready to see what the cards hold next for him in the casino.

Monaco at night. The casino exteriors were filmed two weeks after key interior and gambling scenes in the studios at Leavesden.

to make every dress as sexy and gorgeous as possible.'

The casino scenes need plenty of noise. Director Martin Campbell, who always leaps around the set with great vitality and excitement, tells the extras: 'You are sounding dull and sloppy. Let's hear the background as if you are enjoying yourselves.'

Pierce, who moves his jaw from side to side and bends his legs before every scene to feel more relaxed, finally makes his entrance as Bond, immaculately dressed in black evening suit. Despite instructions to the contrary, all the girls instantly stop talking to look at him.

'For Christ's sake,' says an agitated Martin Campbell, after shouting 'cut'. 'It's not God walking in. He had to make his entrance into what must be the world's only non-speaking casino. Let's go again.'

After that, the words are delivered faultlessly by Brosnan, along with several pages of dialogue and much complex card-playing on games he readily admits he does not really understand.

'Some days are rough and I lose confidence, lose power, lose everything and feel as if I am standing there naked,' he says afterwards.

'I felt that today could have been one of them. There was one point in there, facing Famke (Xenia) across the card table and all the extras in my eyeline, I could feel that things could have gone very wrong.

'But I felt good and strong. Another big dialogue scene is out of the way and I look forward to some action.'

'Shaken not stirred': Bond's famous drink of Vodka Martini, shaken not stirred, is officially listed in Ian Fleming's book, *Casino Royale*, as follows: 'Three measures of Gordons, one of vodka, half a measure of Kina Lillet. Shake it very well until it's ice-cold, then add a large thin slice of lemon peel.' On *GoldenEye*, it was nothing stronger than iced water.

27 February 1995

There is an uneasy atmosphere in Port de Monaco, Monte Carlo. The boundless optimism of expecting non-stop sunshine in February has given way to grudgingly staring at the cloudy skies, which do not match the blue from yesterday afternoon when the scene was started.

Pierce, staying at the Abela Hotel, one mile from the location, is told to wait in his luxurious caravan, which has been brought to the harbourside. He has been able to entertain his eleven-year-old son Sean and his mother May, who have visited on this, only the second of locations outside Leavesden Airfield.

The news from the mountains, where a French car stunt driving team is enacting a race scene between Bond's DB5 and a Ferrari, driven by Xenia, is also not good. A blanket of snow covers the roads and stunt co-

Bond Bash: The Ferarri suddenly stalled in the car chase in the South of France and the Aston Martin DB5 crashed into it. There were instant repairs on-set to the aluminium-bodied DB5, and the Ferarri had to be taken seventy-five miles to Monte Carlo to get a new wing fitted.

ordinator Simon Crane reports there has been a slight collision between the two cars: 'Nothing serious,' he reassures.

'Days like these make you appreciate the security of filming inside Leavesden,' says producer Michael G. Wilson, with one eye on spiralling costs of a film which set out at around $50 million. 'I dare not think about the cost of one wasted day out here. Don't ask.'

Pierce is relaxed. He can do nothing about the weather and rightly feels there is no point in becoming

The car chase, with gyroscopic cameras mounted on Xenia's Ferrari, with Bond and Caroline (Serena Gordon) in pursuit.

tense. Besides, he is feeling more like Bond in this location. There are large and gleaming yachts in the harbour, expensively dressed women strolling around the quay and the steady purring sound of sleek German and Italian cars edging forward so their passengers can step out to restaurants nearby.

The last time he was here was for a brief social trip in 1986 during his filming of *The Fourth Protocol* with Cassie: 'We were staying at The Hermitage over there,' he says, pointing to the five-star hotel just fifty yards away.

'I remember seeing a beautiful gold watch at Cartiers and went in to try it on at some point in every day of our three-day stay. It cost £4,000 and I thought: "I am going to buy this watch when the Bond contract is signed."

'But when we had a wrap party after the film finished in England, Cassie had bought me the watch as a present. The attitude was: "If you like to spend money, then spend money. Worry about it later on."

'I'm glad she thought like that, because it is part of the joy of living. You never know what is around the corner, as we both found out.

'So I got the watch, but not the part of Bond on that occasion. Instead, I had a cheque from the *Remington Steele* people to pay for it.'

There is sudden excitement. The forecast is for the cloud cover to clear within half an hour. Pierce needs to be ready. He seems unperturbed by the instant change of pace, from a morning just waiting to having to be word and action perfect.

'You always have to stay in a holding pattern for something like this,' he observes. 'It is a matter of conserving energy and focusing on what has to be done, more so on *GoldenEye* than any other film. The stakes are higher, the expectations are greater and you don't want to cock it up.'

Within what seems like minutes, he's at the controls of a speedboat, dressed in a dark blue blazer. The boat is moored at the quayside, but as it is supposed to have just arrived, a second speedboat backs up and then speeds off, leaving a realistic wake for Bond's boat.

The scene starts the moment the second speedboat is out of shot, with Bond leaping from the boat, racing up a set of steps and pushing through a crowd. He is trying to prevent Xenia stealing an advanced Tiger helicopter from a French warship.

But Pierce is so fast off the boat that his Walther PPK falls from its holster and plops into the sea. A diver has to retrieve it from several feet of water between takes.

He then has to run up the gangway of the warship *La Fayette* in an attempt to stop the helicopter. Before the first rehearsal, Brosnan can't resist posing like a model, turning this way and that, earning a ripple of applause from the extras.

There is no doubt that he's enjoying being Bond. He's good in the role, but definitely seems to have come to terms with the non-stop Press, television and public attention which seems such a vital ingredient of it all.

One actor who did not seem so steady on his feet then loomed into view: Billy J. Mitchell, who played the hapless Admiral Farrell, crushed to death by Xenia's thighs.

Actress Famke Janssen, who told me a few days ago that she had been working out for weeks in her spare time to strengthen her thighs for this scene, has been delivering a very enthusiastic performance.

They had both been working in a $15 million luxury yacht called *Northern Cross*, which has been hired for use as the *Manticore* during filming.

'She had to slap me during the fight scene,' reports Billy. 'With each take the slap became harder. What with that and the crushing, I can hardly stand up.

'The trouble is, I think they might have to shoot it again because it does not quite work!'

13 March 1995

Pierce Brosnan has trained hard for this role. He did weights and daily kick-boxing back in Malibu, California and can feel the benefits as the six-day weeks go by. His co-star Famke Janssen, who plays Xenia, also talks of the advantages. She underwent a gruelling daily routine in a gymnasium ten miles away in her area of Los Angeles.

But whatever the intensity of the training and exercise, there is nothing that can prepare them for what they're about to witness: Eunice Huthart, Famke's stunt double, about to perform her very first stunt.

Eunice, a gritty winner on the television show *Gladiators*, is dressed in an outfit identical to Xenia's

Every scene and each action shot is first discussed then drawn, comic-strip style, as a storyboard. With Xenia's dramatic death,

black action suit. She will be propelled, backwards, at 30 miles an hour, over an 18ft v-shape in a tree.

The tree may be made of a soft, rubbery substance and we are in Studio A at Leavesden on a set which has been dressed as a jungle clearing, but this is a scene which Pierce and Famke watch in fascination. It is also a special moment for Famke: this is how Xenia dies.

Xenia is locked in a fight to the death with Bond, having abseiled from a helicopter to surprise him. She is still held upright from a line to a helicopter, when he twists her body and fires a pistol strapped to her back towards the pilot.

The pilot pushes the helicopter forward in panic, which propels Xenia against the forked limbs of a tree.

Stunt co-ordinator Simon Crane says: 'We have been setting this one up for weeks. I used a power line with various weights, calculating exactly how high and fast the whole thing should be done.

'I worked out the entire scene before putting any of the stunt doubles at risk. Even so, I am more nervous than anyone today.'

After well over an hour in setting up, Eunice is ready to go. There is silence, a loud crack and suddenly she's flying through the air at an incredible pace. Up, over and a perfect landing on an airbed, several feet high, out of camera shot.

The moment the director yells 'cut' there is a spontaneous ripple of applause from the crew and much

being dragged backwards and upwards by a helicopter cable to an unyielding V-shape tree trunk, nothing was left to chance. Stunt girl Eunice Huthart rehearsed the action. Famke Janssen took her place for the final shot.

admiring conversation from Pierce and Famke: 'They take the risks and live with the danger,' he says. 'It looks so realistic, it is agony to watch even from here.'

GoldenEye bosses have an ambivalent attitude to stunts. They recognise their enormous contribution to the success of the film, but do not like to over-emphasise their importance. It might take something away from the magic of movie-making in general, and Bond's invincibility in particular.

But Pierce says: 'It's a vital part of the process and it's reassuring to watch. There is a safety-first policy at all times, and the same applies to me in the action scenes.'

However, there are some things that cannot be anticipated, however detailed the planning. Eunice, who admits to trembling with fear before the first big pull-back, is told: 'Can you do it again? We did not quite get the camera angles right.'

14 March 1995

It is Sean Bean's first day on set as Trevelyan. Pierce, knowing how tense he felt on his first day, immediately makes contact. They play both friends and enemies on *GoldenEye*, so there is a changing relationship on screen, depending what point they are at in filming.

This morning they are on the same side, supposedly at a nerve gas plant in the opening sequence. In reality, the narrow, bare corridors of the disused Rolls-Royce canteen, on the Leavesden site, are being commandeered.

Bean tells Pierce of his script-learning technique: 'I read it a few times from cover to cover,' he says. 'Then I concentrate on the sections I am doing from day to day.

Sean Bean in action on his first day in his role as Alec Trevelyan, filming the pre-title sequence with Pierce Brosnan.

'I stand in the kitchen, drinking a can of lager, with the telly on and the kids around. Otherwise, it can get too intense. It's very important to stay relaxed, isn't it? That's the hardest part of acting.'

Pierce, who warms to Bean's casual, friendly approach away from the cameras, tells him his own news, freshly delivered by the producers – the poster for the film will declare: 'Pierce Brosnan Is James Bond'.

Both Roger Moore and Timothy Dalton were listed 'as' James Bond. Sean Connery was an 'is'. Brosnan is obviously pleased at the decision.

During today's lunch, Pierce has a sitting for Madame Tussaud's the famous waxworks museum in London which houses figures of real-life and fictional people from over the centuries. A team of three sculptors, two photographers, one eye make-up and colouring expert and one wig and hair supervisor and all under the charge of Judy Craig, Head of Portraits.

Judy tells him that in a normal working year a total of thirty-five models are completed for London, with a further twelve for Amsterdam and Warwick Castle. Pierce will have pride of place in London this Autumn, with a Bond film theme background.

He is asked to stand on a turntable and pose, to be photographed and measured from every angle, with jacket both on and off. Pierce is still wondering about how to position himself, with his Walther PPK held back, high and level with his right eye.

'This is the pose,' says Judy Craig. 'Don't move.'

For the next thirty minutes, sets of callipers are used to get each measurement, whether neck size, ground-to-chin or rib cage, absolutely millimetre-perfect. The body will be made in fibre-glass and his face and hands in wax, he is told, with every hair on his wax head set individually.

At the end of the session, Pierce is asked to write in the Madame Tussaud's book of fame: 'You missed one measurement,' he writes, while smiling broadly. 'But … ah, never mind!'

4 April 1995

Alan Cumming, who plays Boris, sits behind his computer screen in the Cuban control centre set, tapping on his keyboard. Away from the camera, a real computer expert does the same thing, so what shows on screen is correct.

Alan has to shout in triumph: 'I'm invincible,' then watch in horror as details change to yell 'No!', in a shocked Russian accent, which is constantly monitored by dialogue coach, Andrew Jack.

But the real computer expert stumbles on one of the takes and receives a verbal blast from director Martin Campbell: 'Come on – get it ★★★★★★★ right,' he shouts. 'Concentrate!'

Pierce Brosnan watches as the tension rises. It's hot on the set, which has been planned and built painstakingly over several months to look as if it has

been carved out of rock.

He has considerable praise for the volatile Campbell: 'He really is carrying this film,' he says. 'His energy level is very good and he keeps the whole thing exciting. Martin gives the film an edge and a bite.'

Pierce's own energy levels have remained remarkably high, and he has now established a daily pattern which he finds works for him.

'The car comes at six o'clock in the morning to pick me up,' he relates. 'I read a couple of newspapers in the car and have a chat to Colin Morris, my driver.

'The moment we get here it's in to hair and make-up and I eat a bowl of fruit, plus fruit juice. That is all I eat in the morning – apples, oranges, grapes, things like that.

'I am on set at eight o'clock to rehearse the scene. Martin clears the set and he's usually having a nervous breakdown, screaming and shouting at people. I try and stay calm and outside the tension.

Alan Cumming as the devious computer wizard Boris Grishenko in the Cuban control centre, with the GoldenEye (right of picture), which can cause so much world mayhem.

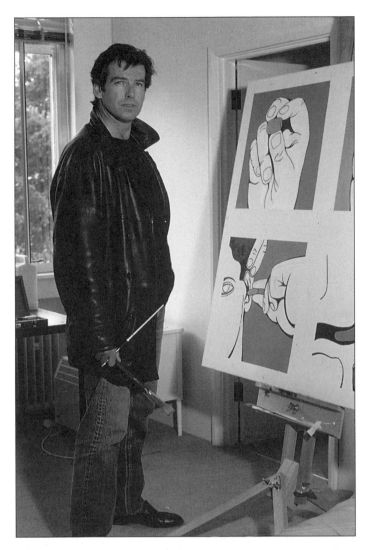

'At lunchtime, I go to my dressing room. I don't lie down, but paint instead. I have my canvasses up. If I had not been an actor, then an artist would have been the next best thing. As it is, I can paint for pleasure without the worry of having to earn a living at it.

'I also do yoga for twenty minutes or so to calm me and clear the mind. In the evening, I try not to have more than a glass or two of wine. It's important to stay fresh. I feel if I let go, then anything could happen.

24 April 1995

The location is the Queen's Stand on Epsom Racecourse, Surrey, which is doubling for the frontage of St Petersburg airport. What's more, it feels like St Petersburg ought to feel. There is a black sky and a slicing, wet, miserable wind; Pierce Brosnan's breath shows white against the icy coldness.

The entrance to the stand is marble, with silver-top stairs and black leather seats. Suitcases and trolleys are added to the wet, cold steps for effect, with a team of extras in rather dowdy Russian clothing.

'It's an odd place to feel as if you're in Russia,' observes Pierce. 'I mean, how much more upmarket can you get than here? Yet it feels so real, doesn't it?'

We all know what he means. This is the scene in which Bond meets his new CIA contact, Jack Wade (Joe Don Baker) for the first time. With the mixture of Russian cars and taxis parked outside, there is the strangest atmosphere of reality.

Yet up a couple of flights of stairs across rich grey carpet is the Queen's Box, which is kept for the exclusive use of the Royal Family on just one race day each year: Derby Day.

The Queen's Box is situated opposite the winning post of the world-famous race and has easy chairs in dark blue, plus a large table, shaped like the cabinet table at 10 Downing Street, with twenty chairs. On the wall are paintings of horses: Cadland, the winner in 1828, St Giles in 1832 and Little Wonder in 1840.

Our guide says that the Queen comments about the colour of the suite every time she makes her annual visit, and insists that she is dazzled because the balcony is so white and bright. One of the Queen's party also brings a toilet cover for her private bathroom.

Next door is the suite owned by Sheikh Al Maktoum, who pays £50,000 a year for eight days' racing and had the place furnished in his own style at a further cost of £40,000. Originally there was a carpet with his initials on, but he insisted that it be replaced because he could not stand anyone walking on his name.

There have been fleeting moments on the movie when the fantastic fictional world of James Bond matches the equally fantastic world of reality. This is one of them.

It is a fight to the death, high above the giant parabolic radio dish. Both Bond and Trevelyan are perfectly matched, having identical training and similar experiences.

16 May 1995

Pierce is forty-two today, and he doesn't feel a day over ninety. Exhausted? No, he says, that's not really the right description. It is a tiredness which sinks in and stays deep inside the body and mind, while outwardly he must remain looking alert and fit.

The twelve-hour days and six-day weeks of dialogue, action, changes and publicity are making him think eagerly of what he regards as a 'finishing line'. 'That is the wrong attitude, because we still have so much to do,' he says.

Pierce has spent most of the day locked in combat with Sean Bean in what will be a long fight sequence at the end of the film. Since it is being filmed in a small space at the top of the scaffolding, Pierce is up and down a long ladder like a hod carrier on a building site.

What's more, he has a 4 pm deadline, a good three hours earlier than usual, to finish the scene. America's top chat show host, David Lettermann, is filming in London and wants to interview the new Bond. With an audience of 30 million, it is thought to be good for the movie.

'I don't want to do it,' says Pierce flatly. 'But the producers and film company thought it was a good idea, so I've agreed. I feel that I ought to get behind the film at every opportunity – that's part of the deal.'

As part of his relaxation exercise at lunchtime Pierce plays for twenty minutes on a clarinet: 'I bought it before Christmas and did not pick it up until today,' he says. 'I learned to play the flute about seven years ago and used that distant memory to get some notes out of it.'

His stand-in and personal assistant, Adrian Bell reports: 'It was bloody awful. But it was a good way for Pierce to let off steam.'

At this low point in the afternoon, Pierce can't resist an observation on the hours he's putting in: 'Six days a week is ridiculous,' he says. 'If you are on a small-budget movie being filmed in seven weeks, then that is more acceptable.

'Over twenty weeks on a movie like this it is a ballbreaker, to be blunt. I fought hard against it before we started and had my say. So, again, I have accepted the situation and it's my job to get on with it.'

Brosnan's pragmatic approach always earns him admiration, and there is a surprise show of appreciation. A cake, in the shape of a Walther PPK, is wheeled in and the entire crew sing 'Happy Birthday'.

Within minutes he's in the back of his driver's Mercedes 420 SEL and Colin Morris is aiming the car towards London: 'We've got one hour to reach the South Bank for the show,' says Colin. 'That's cutting it too fine.'

In fact, they're there with ten minutes to spare. Letterman has a pre-recorded opening gambit that he wants to try on Pierce: 'How about if I walk on and say "The name's David – David Lettermann", and you say, "No, it's more like Pin – Pin Head," ' he suggests.

Pierce agrees. But Lettermann completely forgets himself: "The name is Brosnan – Pierce Brosnan," he says. They quickly do another take before the show.

22 May 1995

The timing, for once, went wrong. Pierce Brosnan arrived on set at 8 am. At one o'clock, he was still dressed in his own black leather jacket and blue sweater, waiting to be called in to wardrobe to prepare for his first scene of the day.

'Come on,' he said. 'Let's go to the pub.'

He had been hearing about this place called The King's Head, a mile or so from the studio, for the last five months. Others had been. He never had the time. Now, he said, it felt like end of term at school. The teachers were still marking books and he had a chance to play.

At Leavesden they were left to struggle on the first unit with a scene at the Cuban control centre, after working with Sean Bean all morning on a spectacular scene featuring his character. They could not call

Pierce, because director Martin Campbell felt that the setting was not quite right and a ladder wasn't falling fast enough.

Over at the second unit on the St Petersburg street things were not going to plan either. One of the Lada cars had been damaged on the inside of a tunnel and there was a hold-up for repairs.

In the pub, Pierce ate cheeseburger and chips and drank two pints of draught lager. It was as if after all the careful eating, cautious drinking and tight self-discipline he could not resist letting go just for an hour or so.

Over the chips and the tomato sauce he talked of his plans: a break in Ireland, back home to Malibu, California and perhaps a holiday in France and Italy: 'I have loved being in this film, but I'd be lying if I said I wasn't ready for a rest,' he says.

'And I am missing the house. I have my business manager and a maid going in every day to deal with bills, business and mess, but it's a long time to be away.'

On his return, there is another delay.

There is no sign of irritation as he leaves to play snooker in the former Rolls-Royce social club with driver Colin Morris: 'I am treating this like an unexpected – but welcome – few hours off,' he says.

25 May 1995

Izabella Scorupco, who plays Natalya, has been called at 7.30 am on her day off to get a shot with Pierce and Sean Bean against a pure blue sky. By the time she has been to hair, make-up and costume department, thick cloud has covered every patch of the much-needed blue and she is being taken home again.

But there is some good news: 'My boyfriend is back with me,' she tells Pierce, with some delight. 'We have a lot of catching up to do.'

Izabella's romance with Polish ice-hockey player Mairusz Czerkwski, who plays in America, had withered and died during the filming of GoldenEye. 'Our relationship is definitely over,' she had announced

Pierce Brosnan can attest that film-making is not all glamour: ten-hour days, six-day weeks for five months. He catches up on news of the outside world – sleeping on the job is not an option.

There is of course a whiff of
romance amid the action. Bond and
Natalya finally get to grips with
each other, rather than the enemy.

only eight weeks before. 'He just could not accept all the time I was spending on this film and wanted me to be with him instead.'

Filming schedules and romance are always a difficult mix. Relationships are often under much pressure with the actors and film crew on *GoldenEye,* and Pierce is the first to recognise it. Reassuringly, he says, his own love affair with American broadcaster Keely Shaye-Smith has survived exactly one year.

'We have been on quite a journey together in that time,' he says. 'She has been good for me and very supportive. You need a lot of understanding from partners in this business if you're going to enjoy anything like a real life away from scripts and cameras.'

Pierce is in action all day, fighting with Sean Bean's character and sliding forcibly down a ladder which is supposedly at the end of the antenna in Cuba. The ladder is propelled, off camera, by one of the special effects team. On the fifth take it shoots down so fast it seems to take his breath away; director Campbell is delighted and immediately orders 'Print that one'.

'I made the mistake of telling the guy in charge of the ladder that he looked a bit like Russ Abbot,' says Pierce, as he nursed an aching back. 'I should have said Mel Gibson.'

Physiotherapist Elaine Juzl and occupational therapist Nicola Goldsmith, who have been giving him thrice-weekly treatment on his injured right hand, join Pierce for lunch. He's a great patient, they say, but he does not have time for enough exercise on the injured hand.

As the day wears on, so does the sore right hand holding the ladder. A glove is used, but appears in shot. Then the glove is used to support only as he 'falls' away from the ladder. It follows his body, again in shot. Finally, a small piece of soft leather is cut and held close to his palm to ease the agony as he grips the steel rung again.

Linda DeVetta, make-up supervisor, automatically sprays his face to give the effect of sweat between takes: 'I don't think we need that,' he mutters. 'The pain on my face is real.'

Bond past meets Bond present. Roger Moore arrives to see Pierce on his final day, joking: 'They sent for me – I'm back on the job.'

1 June 1995

Roger Moore, veteran of seven Bond films, visits the set to see his son, Christian, who has been working as a third assistant, and his old friend, producer Michael G. Wilson.

He is limping from a knee operation after an accident on a recent film in Thailand and greets Pierce with an instant wind-up: 'I've been called up. They said: "We've seen the results on poor old Brosnan, so get the knee right and you're back in the job." '

There is much similar laughter and banter throughout the afternoon as Pierce takes his place in one of the tanks on the St Petersburg set for some tight and twisting manoeuvres.

Moore knows both the pleasure and the strain of being 007. It is a role with public image, responsibility and longevity; there is nothing like it in movie history.

Pierce remains remarkably relaxed. He's lived with the part for exactly a year to the day, in preparation, rehearsal and filming, and there is a feeling of optimism in every quarter.

The film editing department report that it's definitely a winner; there is delight on what has been seen so far from movie giants MGM/UA and the first poster hangs proudly everywhere on Leavesden's walls with a picture of Brosnan, plus gun, and a caption: 'You know the name … You know the number.'

'All I can think about at the moment is: "Did I get it right?" ' says Pierce. 'I replay certain scenes and days in my mind, looking for imperfections. I don't think it is a part I can leave behind, like other films.'

He has finally and most emphatically come to terms with the long wait to play the part that he was first given in 1986. It would have haunted him forever if he hadn't won the right to play 007 second time around. The frustration, the anger and the questions have been laid to rest.

But there is also serious reflection and an admission that perhaps fate took a hand after all: 'I feel much better equipped to play the role, both as a man and an actor,' he says. 'In 1986 I was quite fearful about the part. The script sat by my bed and I never read it.

'I could not bring myself to read it until the contract was signed. Of course it was never signed due to those awful circumstances and the script lay unread.

'Now, people are saying: "Yes, you are doing it at last." I can feel their warmth and enthusiasm and expectation, because I am current tenant of the most famous film role in the world. And I love it.'

Tank Man. Bond takes over the huge T55 Russian tank for the spectacular chase sequence.

THE GOOD, THE BAD, THE UGLY ... AND Q

THE GOOD

JAMES BOND

GOLDENEYE DESCRIPTION   *Does not need any.*

ACTOR: PIERCE BROSNAN

Aged forty-two, strikingly handsome, artistic, with a strong belief in close family life. In fifteen years has gone from a silent debut as an IRA hired killer opposite Bob Hoskins in the final scene of *The Long Good Friday* to the world's most famous secret agent. His relaxed, polite manner belies a fierce ambition. Moved from County Meath, Ireland to London with his family in 1963, aged ten. Began his career as acting assistant stage manager at the York Theatre Royal, but six months later was selected by Tennessee Williams to create the role of McCabe in *The Red Devil Battery Sign*. It made London's West End theatre world sit up and take note. After a series of TV roles, he risked all by moving to Hollywood without a job. It paid off with *Remington Steele* and the NBC mini series *Noble House*. Ironically, his big film break came playing a crack Soviet agent in *The Fourth Protocol*, from Frederick Forsyth's bestseller. Has since starred in a string of box office hits, including *The Lawnmower Man* and *Mrs Doubtfire*.

On his role: 'I never sat down to think: I have to be different. He is a commander, drinks the drink, gets the girl, talks to the boss and goes into highly dangerous situations. I did not want to look at all that and think of a special twist or an angle. We have had thirty-three years and two or three generations of an audience who have grown up with Bond. I wanted to keep him simple, direct, honest and as exciting as possible.'

On himself: 'I brought my youngest son Sean aged eleven with me to London and he went to the American School and my eldest son, Christopher has been third assistant director on the film's second unit. My daughter Charlotte has been in and out of London and we have seen each other every time. All this has been great support for me. When my wife Cassie died in 1989 a light went out in my life and I put great store in the family. We all have our needs. I need mine'.

On Bond: 'There is such a love for this character, established by Sean Connery and Roger Moore, and I

think a lot of people are hungry to see the role succeed. I do not think we have to compete with other action films. As great as some of them are, they're not Bond.'

NATALYA SIMONOVA

GOLDENEYE DESCRIPTION
A striking young woman in her twenties, slender, very sexy in an unselfconscious way.

ACTRESS: IZABELLA SCORUPCO

Born in 1970 in a North-East Polish village called Byalystok, close to the Russian border. Moved, aged eight, with her doctor mother Magdalena to Stockholm, Sweden. Film debut aged seventeen, worked as a model, became a successful singer, then returned to acting last year.

On her role: 'I think it is the first time you see a Bond girl looking messy and vulnerable throughout most of the film. I am messed up in the opening scene and she hardly has a change of clothes, because she's in so much action. But she can stand up for herself and is an independent, intelligent woman.'

On herself: 'I had trouble with my Polish boyfriend and we broke up during most of the film. He is an ice hockey player in Boston and felt that really I should be at home with him rather than in the arms of James Bond. I had been loyal and faithful and it was a very silly split. But he realised his mistake just a couple of weeks before GoldenEye finished filming and we are back together again.'

On Bond: 'The first time Pierce and I filmed together, we had to kiss on a beach because it is near the end of the movie and our characters know each other very well. It was difficult, so I told him: "I have to sit and watch you for two hours, because I want to see how you act." He was very easy to watch and work with. A very handsome man, but a real gentleman too.'

JACK WADE

GOLDENEYE DESCRIPTION
A burly-looking American CIA man with a rose-shaped tattoo emblazoned 'Muffy' on his upper right hip, in tribute to his third wife.

ACTOR: JOE DON BAKER

Constantly in demand character actor, sixty next year. Born in Texas, swept to fame with the 1972 movie *Walking Tall* playing a small-town Tennessee sheriff and has enjoyed a string of hit movies. Notable as one of the few actors to appear in two Bond films, playing different parts. He appeared as Whitaker, a powerful international arms dealer, in the fifteenth Bond, *The Living Daylights*.

On his role: 'He's a hell of a guy, a real fun man. I don't suppose he is your typical CIA agent. He's a bit of a rogue and an independent thinker. They probably treat him as a rebel and this is why he has to suffer life in Russia.

On himself: 'I became so sick and tired of Hollywood and all the pomposity, at one point I was ready to pack it all in. So I try and keep moving on films like this. It's the fifth film I have out this year and it's easy to be in a daze.'

On Bond: 'I saw *Dr No* when I was in New York studying acting and I've always had a soft spot for the films. Pierce is going to be a hit, because he is both macho and stylish. I would like to be part of any future Bonds with this character, if possible, particularly as he's no goody two-shoes. Bond has appeal because of great looking girls and a licence to kill which we all might like once in a while. Everyone would like to drive the cars, do the stunts and have the women, but 99.9 per cent of us don't have the nerve.'

THE BAD

XENIA ONATOPP

GOLDENEYE DESCRIPTION
Tall, beautiful, dressed in black, with muscular legs and an unusual sexual appetite, which includes crushing her lovers to death with her thighs.

ACTRESS: FAMKE JANSSEN

Dutch-born 5ft 11inches tall former model, aged twenty-nine who has lived in America for the past eleven years. Majored in writing and literature at Columbia University. TV roles in *Star Trek*, *Melrose Place* and *The Untouchables*. Film debut in *Fathers and Sons*, opposite Jeff Goldblum. Debut starring role in Clive Barker supernatural thriller – also MGM/UA film – *Lord of Illusions*.

On her role: 'Xenia liberated me. I do not have that excitement about life as she does. Everything is a thrill to her and she's a joy to play. Of course, she's a thrill junkie who is also dangerous and happens to enjoy killing people. It is me, if I could go completely mad for a day! She has grown up in Russia, with shortages and little money. So she's like a child in a sweet shop, with a bag full of gold coins.'

On herself: 'I lived in New York with my Dutch boyfriend of five and a half years. Then I met my husband, Todd Williams and fell madly in love at first sight. I was on an assignment in the Bahamas, so thought it must have been the setting and the situation. But I could not get him out of my mind and proposed marriage. It was the one time I have acted totally on impulse.'

On Bond: 'The director, Martin Campbell, was always open to suggestions and wanted to make Xenia an exciting prospect. I added the fact she smoked cigars and used it as an extra prop. But I got a little carried away on the scenes with Billy J. Mitchell, who played the Admiral, when I was supposed to crush him to death in my thighs. The night before, I was worried about doing the scene, dressed in black corset and stockings. But in the end it was so risqué that we had to do it all over again on another day.'

ALEC TREVELYAN

GOLDENEYE DESCRIPTION
Fast. Ruthless. Fit. A match for Bond. The right side of his face is marked by a skin graft, the left side of his mouth frozen.

ACTOR: SEAN BEAN

A former welder from Sheffield, Yorkshire, who at thirty-six emerged as one of Britain's biggest action-man sex symbols. Changed his working lifestyle by joining the prestigious RADA (Royal Academy of Dramatic Arts), where he won the Silver Medal, plus two fencing awards. Films include *Stormy Monday*, *The Field* and *Patriot Games*. Television impact as dastardly Lovelace in *Clarissa*, Mellors in *Lady Chatterley's Lover* and as the eponymous hero of *Sharpe*.

On his role: 'I don't see him as evil. He believes what he is doing is the right thing to do. He sees Bond as old-fashioned and asks him to question why he has killed so many people in the line of duty. Trevelyan says that at last he admits he's doing wrong and has no qualms about it. I imagine his background as public school, Sandhurst and consistent mixture of intense education and the very best military training.'

On himself: 'I'm like many people who look at actors and think: "I'd like to be doing his job." ' The difference is that today I am lucky enough to be doing it. That means shooting guns, swinging punches, kissing beautiful women, playing interesting people – and being paid for it. I go home at the end of the day and shut off with my wife Melanie Hill, who is also an actress, and our two daughters. When I can, I go and watch Sheffield United football team with my mates and they will always ask: "What's so-and-so like?" '

On Bond: 'I saw Dr No as a little kid and I've enjoyed the films ever since. Pierce and I both wanted to make this as hard and dangerous as possible, so we would be hitting the hell out of each other, then meeting up for a sip of Irish whiskey at his house at night. He's acted the part superbly.'

GENERAL ARKADY GRIGOROVICH OURUMOV

GOLDENEYE DESCRIPTION

A founder member of the mysterious Janus Syndicate. Iron man of Russia: tough, cold, calculating.

ACTOR: GOTTFRIED JOHN

Distinguished German actor, classically trained at Berlin's Dramatic Art School and experienced stage performer – with leading Shakespeare roles such as Macbeth and Richard III – long before his film debut. Five German films directed by Reiner Werner Fassbinder and British TV dramas such as *The Night of the Fox* and *Game, Set and Match*.

On his role: 'He is a traditional Russian General who tries to re-establish the old system, while using the new Russian mafia to do so. He ends up being destroyed by people who are even stronger than he is. I tried to make him believable and not just someone who is bad. The audience should understand this

character: he thinks he can win the battle, but becomes like a trapped animal.'

On himself: 'I was born in Berlin but have since lived in Bavaria, France and now with my wife in Belgium. It is a nice and pretty place, but I never work there. I worked hard at the start of my career to fight against playing bad-guy roles. I look big and mean, so they look at my face and say: nasty. The truth is rather different and my wife and I take in stray cats and look after them.'

On Bond: 'He has lasted so long, because he was the first regular action hero in film history. This time, he is a sensible Bond and Pierce has brought a new and interesting angle to his character. He has made him very human.'

THE UGLY

VALENTIN ZUKOVSKY

GOLDENEYE DESCRIPTION

A burly, moon-faced man in a voluminous white linen suit; a former KGB Controller turned ruthless Russian arms dealer.

ACTOR: ROBBIE COLTRANE

Big, unconventional, witty. Unusual boast is that he can detect – and speak – 300 separate British accents. Born in 1950, trained at Glasgow School of Art. At twenty-three he produced and directed award-winning fifty minute documentary called *Young Mental Health*. Toured American universities with San Quentin Theatre Workshop in mid-Seventies. Famous in Britain for Comic Strip performances, then hit TV series like *Tutti Frutti* (with Emma Thompson) and *Cracker*, in which he plays criminal psychologist Fitz.

On his role: 'I have always wanted to play the main

baddie in a Bond film and Valentin is the next best thing. I did not get a pussy cat to stroke, but it's still good. There's some good dialogue and a strong tongue-in-cheek element, but it's a straight part.'

On himself: 'I have always been a movie fan and when you consider how bad TV was in the Sixties, that's not surprising. I've got a son (aged three in December, 1995) who is already keen. He's watching *The Wild One*, a video lent to us by Emma Thompson. He keeps on saying: "I want to watch the man on the motorbike, daddy." So there's plenty of hope for him.'

On Bond: 'The first Bond I saw was *Dr No* with my dad when I was thirteen. I remember Ursula Andress walking out of the sea and the place went mad. I always wanted to be James Bond – all that sex and having a licence to kill people. Something all young boys aspire to! We used to leap up and down in the streets and I would imagine having a DB5 and going to a casino and knowing exactly what to do. Bond knows what wine to order, how to drive and how to chat up girls. He'll last forever.'

and *Black Beauty* – as the voice of the horse.

On his role: He's a funny baddie. I quite like him, because he's bizarre and evil at the same time. I tried to combine a Russian dourness and American computer geek awareness. I have added a pair of spectacles to him and wear my hair really greasy. I also wear some shorts in the Cuban bunker.'

On himself: 'I have played a lot of nice boys in the past. Even in my first job, as a writer for a teen magazine, I was used for photographs in those picture stories about romance. I was the nice guy who never got the girl. But recently things have changed. I was even with Samantha Bond, who plays Moneypenny, in a TV drama where we had to simulate a sex scene in the back of a taxi.'

On Bond: 'It's a strange feeling to be finally in one, like being a wee boy wanting to drive a fire engine and at last being behind the wheel. But from Day One, there was a feeling of being in something incredible, and everyone knows their job inside out.'

BORIS IVANOVICH GRISHENKO

GoldenEye Description
Edgy, imperious, wild-haired cyberpunk in his mid-twenties, wearing a Wired magazine logo T-shirt under his black leather motorcycle jacket rife with zippers and snaps.

ACTOR: ALAN CUMMING

Much lauded and awarded thirty-year old Scottish actor, writer and director. Won British Comedy Award for Top Television Newcomer in 1992 and has been collecting awards regularly since. Film appearances include *Prague* (Best Actor, 1992 Atlantic Film Festival), *Circle Of Friends*

DIMITRI MISHKIN

GoldenEye Description
Sober-suited, middle-aged, with fingers impatiently drumming on a table as he waits.

ACTOR: TCHEKY KARYO

French star who has occasionally crossed barriers to make international impact. The Luc Besson film, *Nikita*, one example; Ridley Scott's *1492* another, plus the recent *Nostradamus*. Born 4 October 1953. Classic stage roles and French arthouse films.

On his role: 'Mishkin is one of the younger generation of politicians. An elegant, smart man, very ambitious. Fights against the military trying to take over Russia.

On himself: 'I am not as serious as I look – and neither is Bond. I consider myself born into a melting pot. My Turkish father spoke French with a pronounced accent, a little like Russian, and that has been useful to remember in this. That voice of his would be perfect for it.'

On Bond: 'There is so much action and humour and Bond is a character that a lot of people love. Each time a Bond movie is coming up, there is a great feeling of entertainment. Pierce has a lightness of humour and he seems very British, with the quality as Bond that we will all appreciate.'

… AND Q

GoldenEye Description
Needs no introduction.

ACTOR: DESMOND LLEWELYN

Warm and talkative and immensely likeable. He's become an institution on the strength of one part and is recognised throughout the world. He had been in the movie business for twenty-four years – his 1939 debut was in a Will Hay comedy, *Ask A Policeman* – before he was first seen on screen as Q in *From Russia With Love*. Has appeared as MI6's gadget inventor in every Bond film apart from the first, *Dr No*, and *Live And Let Die*.

On his role: 'Q would probably not like to see a foreign car, the BMW, used by Bond and he would not approve of a female M, either. That's how he is: old fashioned in a changing world. The first director Terence Young wanted me to do the part as a Welshman. I had been in one of his films, *They Were Not Divided*, playing a Welsh tank driver and he thought the same accent would work. I knew it wouldn't. Once I

The accents: *GoldenEye's* voice coach, Andrew Jack, said he's never had a job like it. He was in constant attendance to make sure that the cast playing Russians had a uniformity about their accents. But what made it such a challenge was that with an international cast, they spoke with a wide variety of dialects. Famke Janssen (Xenia) is Dutch; Izabella Scorupco (Natalya), Polish (living in Sweden); Gottfried John (Ourumov) is German and Tcheky Karyo (Mishkin) French. Alan Cumming (Boris) and Robbie Coltrane (Valentin) are both Scottish. 'Before we got around to Russian, my first task was to get them talking with a uniformity in English,' says Jack.

delivered the first speech he said: "You were right. Now speak English." '

On himself: 'My recognition far outstrips my importance or wealth, and sometimes people seem to think I should be travelling in smart cars and having exotic holidays instead of shopping in the local supermarket. People always seem to notice me, but are very kind. I was having a pub lunch the other day with my wife when Bond music from *Moonraker* came on in the background. One of the other customers said: "They must have put this on for you." No-one had said a thing to me up to then. It's a great ice-breaker and conversation point.'

On Bond: 'The question I am always asked is: "Which is the best?" The answer is: "Whoever you saw first." In some areas of America, they prefer Roger to Sean because he's smooth and funny. There were those who did not like Tim Dalton because he was too real. Others felt Tim was the best Bond and the closest to Ian Fleming's version. Roger was always a good friend to me and was a constant teaser, but from watching all the films – if I had to have my arm twisted – I would say Sean Connery was my personal favourite. Watch Pierce Brosnan, though. He may just be the best yet.'

M AND HER BOND GIRLS

The *GoldenEye* script introduces the first female M as 'late forties who by her very presence and stride commands respect.' Dame Judi Dench, chosen for the role, says: 'It's one of the most flattering invitations I've ever had.

'I was sixty last December, but the director Martin Campbell wrote to me offering me the part. I have always adored the really unexpected and this was certainly it. What's more, he obviously thinks I am much younger than I am.'

Dame Judi has brought a new style to Bond. Miss Moneypenny, played by Samantha Bond, is seen wearing an elegant black dress on her way out for the evening. And M's other Bond girl, Caroline – played by Serena Gordon – is dressed in designer clothes.

There is an upmarket feel, an indication that this M will bring in her own women. It also gives the film a classic look, which moves imperceptibly further away from the Bond Girl image.

Judi has always been a Bond follower: 'What was it about Connery in the early days?' she asks. 'Sex – written in letters large! He has enormous appeal and set the standards which have been kept up over more than thirty years. It is an incredible achievement.

'But the only reason for continuing success is that the producers and directors have been able to capture the mood of the times. There is very much a "new man" around now, so it is no use going back to the attitudes of the early Sixties.

'Morality was very different then and we were not so aware of the changing world. Women in business

Moneypenny, called in for a late-night emergency conference, obviously has a life of her own outside MI6. With a nicely ironic, touch, Samantha Bond plays Moneypenny.

weren't treated with respect and very few of them could make their mark at the top.

'There is now a woman at the head of the British Secret Service and this Bond film reflects that — quite rightly, in my view. In turn, M would not employ bimbos around her, but intelligent, successful girls.'

Judi also mirrors the underlying mood of Bond films, which do not fall into the trap of being politically correct: 'I do not call myself a feminist,' she says.

'I like it when a man opens a door for me or stands up when I walk in to a room. I love all that. And as someone who has worked alongside men all her life — as an equal, I am glad to say — I find that is the view of the vast majority of all women.

'I get to call Bond a sexist and have a real go at him. I enjoyed that scene enormously and so did Pierce. He had to sit there and take it, while I worried about how I

was sounding.

'I may just break a habit of a lifetime with *GoldenEye*. I have never watched myself on film — I absolutely hate it — but know in my heart that I won't be able to resist watching this one.'

Judi brought an impressive pedigree to the set. She received an OBE (Order of the British Empire) in 1970 for services to theatre; in 1988 she became a DBE (Dame of the British Empire), having performed virtually all of the great classic roles on stage.

She was playing Ophelia in *Hamlet* and Maria in *Twelfth Night* at the Old Vic nearly forty years ago, and has won twenty-one awards — including five British Academy Awards in her career.

So she carries a great deal of weight when giving her own verdict on the new Bond: 'Pierce Brosnan is definitely the man for the job,' she says. 'He has all the manners and attitudes we have been talking about. He has huge sex appeal, but is genuinely charming, likes women as people and is relaxed in our company. He brings that attitude to the screen.'

Director Campbell purposely hired actresses to complement Dame Judi as M. Samantha Bond, certainly blessed with the right name for an 007 film, plays Miss Moneypenny, again after several heavyweight roles at the Royal Shakespeare Company.

'In this, Moneypenny is like a sparring partner for Bond and with M being a woman, the emphasis is on strength and femininity,' she says. 'But glamour is just as important.

'I remember seeing Ursula Andress coming out of the sea while watching *Dr No* on TV and thinking: "How marvellous." I was never worried in the slightest about Bond films being sexist.

'At the time of Sean Connery, all women in films were portrayed in more or less the same way. But it is very impressive the way this new film moves on with the mood of the moment, while not losing the banter and light-heartedness of Bond's attitude to women.

'Bond is also an historical fantasy. I can't think of anyone I know in the acting business who would not leap at a chance of a part. And the impact is unbelievable. After the press launch in January, I had a call from an aunt in Norway to say she'd watched the whole thing on television.

'With Moneypenny comes all that history and responsibility. But since I have lived with Bond jokes all my life, because of my name, it was great to be officially part of it all.'

Although he had no way of knowing, Campbell guessed right about the background of M's girls. Samantha, educated at Godolphin and Latymer school in Hammersmith, London, went to the prestigious Bristol Old Vic drama school.

Serena Gordon, who plays Caroline and is introduced as 'a beautiful young woman of impeccable background', boarded at Bryanston, in Blandford, Dorset and then won a place at RADA. Her character, immaculately dressed and groomed, is sent to conduct an evaluation report on Bond.

'My friends have been falling around with laughter at the prospect of me being a Bond girl,' she says disarmingly. 'I think they are expecting to see me in a bikini rather than Armani.

'But my nineteen-year-old brother Jamie, who is a huge Bond fan and was in Alice Springs, Australia when I got the part, was so excited. He phoned in and said it was like a dream come true.'

Serena, who has a strong theatre background, has also been in TV series like *Riders*, *Kinsey* and the comedy based on the Royal Family, *The House of Windsor*.

'I think it's great that we don't see huge amounts of naked flesh in Bond,' she says. 'But it is pretty obvious in the script that Caroline is going to be swept off her feet when Bond serves her from a chilled bottle of Bollinger in his Aston Martin DB5. So he has not lost his touch …'

Caroline, the M girl sent to 'evaluate' Bond, is played by Serena Gordon.

AND ... ACTION

It is the moment of truth. The actors line up to deliver the action. But what do they have to work with? Here is the original script for four key scenes in GoldenEye.

First, Bond is with Miss Moneypenny in M's outer office. Then he has his first confrontation with the new M at MI6. Later, he is briefed by old favourite, Q. Next, he meets new CIA contact Jack Wade at St Petersburg airport. (Script © Danjaq, Inc.)

107 INT. MI6 HEADQUARTERS. M's OUTER OFFICE, NIGHT.

MONEYPENNY, hair done up and dressed to thrill in a little black number, stands up from her desk as Bond enters.

BOND Good evening, Moneypenny.

MONEYPENNY M will meet you in the situation room. I'm to take you straight in.

She picks up encoded key card from her desk.

108 INT. MI6 HEADQUARTERS, CORRIDOR/FOLLOWING NIGHT.

Bond and Moneypenny, walking. He looks her over, registering surprise.

BOND   I've never seen you, after hours, Moneypenny. Lovely.

MONEYPENNY   Thank you, James.

BOND   Out on some kind of professional assignment? Dressing to kill?

They reach an elevator. She swipes the card in a reader, and eyes him wryly:

MONEYPENNY … I know you'll find it crushing 007, but I do not sit home every night praying for some kind of international incident so I can run down here all perfumed up to impress James Bond.

The elevator door opens. As she gets in:

MONEYPENNY   I was on a date, if you must know.

108A   INT. ELEVATOR
Two sets of doors – the ones they've just entered, another they'll go out. She continues:

MONEYPENNY   … With a gentleman. We went to the theatre together.
BOND   Moneypenny! I'm devastated! What would I ever do without you?

MONEYPENNY   So far as I can remember, you've never had me, James.

BOND   Hope springs eternal.

She cocks her head, with amusement:

MONEYPENNY   You know, this kind of behaviour could qualify as sexual harassment.

BOND   And what's the penalty for that?

The elevator doors open.

MONEYPENNY   Some day you have to make good on your innuendoes.

Bond motions to the open elevator door, but means something else entirely:

BOND   After you, Moneypenny.

MONEYPENNY   No. I insist. You first.

A beat. Bond goes. Moneypenny smiles, and follows.

* * * * * *

130   INT. MI6 HEADQUARTERS. M's OFFICE. NIGHT.

Bond and M, who is on the phone.

M   (into phone) Very well sir … yes, goodnight.

M hangs up the phone.

M   The Prime Minister's talked with Moscow. They're saying it was an accident during a routine training exercise.

BOND Governments change, the lies stay the same.

She registers this, but lets it slide.

M What else do we know about the Janus Syndicate?

BOND Top-flight arms dealers, headquartered in St Petersburg. First outfit to re-stock the Iraqis during the Gulf War. Head man's unreliably described; no photographs. The woman, Onatopp, is our only confirmed contact.

M takes this in. She looks out the window.

M Would you care for a drink?

BOND Thank you. Your predecessor kept some Cognac –

M (moved to the liquor cabinet) I prefer bourbon. Ice?

Bond nods, watching her. She hands him the drink.

M We pulled the files on anyone who might have had access – or authority – at Severnaya ...

She looks at a piece of paper on her desk.

M The top name on the list is an old friend of yours.

She presses a button, and a large monitor is revealed in the wall. A photograph of Ourumov in full uniform appears, his data logged underneath.

BOND (after a moment, evenly) Ourumov. They've made him a general.

M He sees himself as the next Iron Man of Russia. Which is why our political analysts rule him out. He doesn't fit the profile of a traitor.

BOND Are those the same analysts who said GoldenEye couldn't exist? … Who said the helicopter posed no immediate threat, and wasn't worth following?

She puts down her drink. Studies Bond, and – very calmly, and matter-of-factly –

M You don't like me, Bond. You don't like my methods. You think I'm an accountant – a bean counter – who's more interested in my numbers than your instincts.

BOND The thought had occurred to me.

M Good. Because I think you're a sexist, misogynist dinosaur. A relic of the cold war … Whose boyish charms, I might add, although lost on me … Obviously appealed to that young woman I sent out to evaluate you.

BOND Point taken.

M Not quite, 007. (pause) If you think – for one moment – that I don't have the balls to send a man out to die, your instincts are dead wrong.

She pauses. Bond, impassive.

M I have no compunction about sending you to your death. But I won't do it on a whim. Even with your cavalier attitude about life.

Almost off-handedly, Bond explains the way he lives his life:

BOND … I've never forgotten that a licence to kill is also a certificate to die.

M nods.

M I want you to find GoldenEye. I want you to find who took it, what they plan to do with it, and stop it. (beat, glancing at the monitor) And if you do run across Ourumov – guilty or not – I don't want you running off on some kind of vendetta. Avenging Alec Trevelyan will not bring him back.

She nods; the interview is over. She turns back to the work on her desk. He walks to the door without looking back until he hears –

M   Bond – (he turns to see her. Then:) Come back alive

* * * * * *

131 INT. MI6 HEADQUARTERS. Q's WORKSHOP. DAY

Boffins at work on various projects – including two men aiming a cannon-like gun at a third. They fire it – and the man is enveloped in a taffy-like riot control substance that he can't pull out of. Bond finds:
Q in a wheelchair, one leg extended in a full cast. Bond follows alongside him.

BOND   Sorry about your leg, Q.

Q   Hmmm?

BOND   Skiing?

Suddenly, the foot of the cast drops open and a rocket fires across the workshop and through a leaded curtain, exploding into the far wall. Bond looks agape. Q looks up at him, deadpan:

Q   Hunting.

Q rolls his eyes, slips off the cast, stands, and leads Bond across the room, passing a BMW sports coupé that several men are outfitting with Q improvements.

Q   Now pay attention 007.

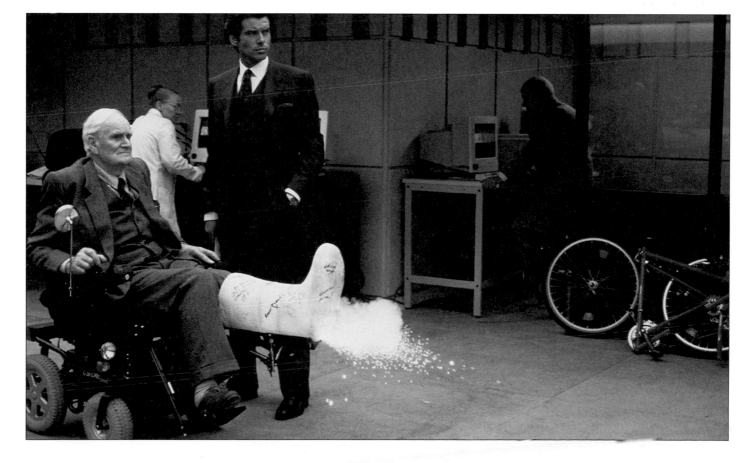

(points to the car)
First, your new car. BMW. Agile.
Highly refined. Six forward gears,
all-points radar, self-destruct
system, stinger missiles behind the
headlamps.

BOND … Just the thing for unwinding
after a rough day at the office.

Q Need I remind you, 007 you have a
licence to kill – not break traffic
laws?

BOND I wouldn't think of it.

Q Good, Now let's move on to more
practical matters.

He has led Bond to a bench where his
new toys are laid out, along with an
array of test monitors. BOND LAYS HIS
ENVELOPE DOWN ON A SILVER TEA SERVICE
TRAY. Ever-curious, his eyes begin to
wander.

Q picks up an ordinary looking men's
leather belt.

Q A typical leather belt. Male. Size
34. Buckle, notch – (sees Bond isn't
listening)
Ahem.

BOND (brought up short) Yes?

Q A typical leather belt. Male. Size
34. Buckle notch –

BOND (interrupting) Q: I'm familiar
with the device.

Q – not with a 75 foot rappelling
cord built into the buckle.
(explaining)
Aim here, fire here, and a piton
shoots out followed by a high tensile
wire designed to support your weight.

BOND And if I need additional
support?

Q It's tested for one, 007.

Q looks around the table for his next
toy. He spots the envelope on the
silver tea-service tray. With an
irritated frown, he hands it to Bond.

Q Seat 7-A, British Airways to Saint
Petersburg.

Bond is baffled. Q holds up the silver
tray.
Q X-ray document scanner.

He points to one of the test monitors,
where Bond sees the information. Q,
meanwhile, has picked up a pen:

Q Next: This pen looks like a pen,
works like a pen, Click once to
write, once to retract.

BOND Ingenious.

Q … We're working on a version that
will provide you with wit.
(beat)
In the meantime, this is a class 4
grenade. Three clicks, you arm its
four-second fuse, three more,
disarms it.

Bond takes the pen, clicks three times and waits.

BOND How long did you say the fuse was?

Q snatches back the pen - clicks three times to disarm it.

Q Shorter than mine.

BOND They always said the pen was mightier than the sword.

Q And they were right.

Bond, is puzzled; Q takes the pen across the room to a mannequin dressed in a white laboratory coat.

Q Let's ask our friend Freddie here to demonstrate.

He clicks the pen, tucks it in the mannequin's lab coat chest pocket. He walks back and stands next to Bond.

The pen explodes, obliterating the top of the mannequin, leaving it a charred smoking mess. Q eyes an amused Bond.

Q Don't say it.

BOND The handwriting was on the wall?

Q Along with the rest of him.
(beat)

Now 007, do try and return some of this equipment in pristine condition. The budget? Even the Queen pays taxes these days.

Bond picks up a French-stick sandwich from the bench.

BOND What does this do?

Q (in alarm) Don't touch that.

Carefully Bond sets it down. Q picks it up, takes a bite.

Q That's my lunch.

* * * * * *

144B   EXT. ST PETERSBURG. AIRPORT RUNWAY. DAY.

The daily British Airways flight from London touching down.

144C   EXT. ST PETERSBURG AIRPORT. TERMINAL ENTRANCE. DAY.

Bond comes out of the terminal and walks to a taxi queue. Well-dressed businessmen get into cars. Directly ahead of Bond is a burly-looking American, Jack Wade, casually paging through a Russian gardening magazine.

Bond and Wade glance at each other.

BOND (recognition code) ... In London, April is a spring month.

Wade lowers the magazine and chuckles cynically:
What're you? The weatherman?

A moment. Bond cautious. Then Wade laughs:

I mean. Jesus Christ. Another stiff-assed Brit with your secret codes and your passwords - one day you guys are gonna just learn to drop it.
(starts to walk off)

C'mon. The car's over there.
Bond cautiously follows as Wade leads in the direction of a shiny chauffeur-driven Mercedes ...

Which drives off, revealing a junky, battered Moskvich.

144D   NEW ANGLE -

As Wade approaches the door -

BOND   Allow me -

And Bond opens the door. Wade starts to get in, but Bond wedges the door against Wade's bulk. Wade reacts with surprise.

BOND   As you said - drop it.

Wade looks down at Bond's Walther, embedded in his ribs. But instead of fright, Wade reacts with chagrin, pleading:

WADE   C'mon –

Bond doesn't react; Wade struggles to remember the code. Then:

WADE   A'right: In London April is a spring month, while in St Petersburg we're still freezing our butts off. Close enough?

BOND   No. Show me the rose.

WADE   Jesus H. Christ.

Shielded from onlookers by the door, (and with great reluctance) Wade loosens his belt, and shows a ROSE-SHAPED TATTOO emblazoned 'MUFFY' on his left upper hip.

BOND   … Muffy?

WADE   Third wife. (grins, extends a hand) Jack Wade, CIA.

BOND   (shakes it, amused) James Bond. Stiff-assed Brit.

WADE   Nice move.

BOND   Nice car.

WADE   (defensively) Hey – you have any idea what the CIA is paying us agents these days?

As Bond walks to the passenger door:

BOND   To the penny. Your last defector gave an interview to the Moscow Times.

Wade sniggers. Pats the roof of the car:

WADE   Well … This baby's never let me down. Ugly son-of-a-bitch, but she gets you there. (gesturing with the magazine) You do any gardening?

Bond reacts – this guy truly is nuts. They get in the car, and on the door slam we

CUT TO:

144E   EXT. ST PETERSBURG SQUARE. DAY.

Panning down from the glorious architecture, we find …

Wade's Moskvich, bonnet propped open, Wade bent over, working on the engine.

WADE   Wanna hand me that wrench Jimmy?

Bond reaches into the bright red tool box, hands it to him.

BOND   So what do you know about Janus?

WADE   Zilch. Zipsky. Pliers? (Bond hands them down) Nobody's ever seen him, but the man's connected up to the kazoo. Military. KGB. Screwdriver. (again, Bond hands it) Rumour has it he lives on one of those old Soviet missile trains – armoured stuff they used to run around the country so we couldn't target 'em.
He stands for a moment, wipes his brow.

WADE Wanna give me that hammer?

Bond reaches for a small hammer –

WADE No. The bigger one. The sledge.

Bond hands him a 3½ lb sledge hammer. Wade goes back to work under the bonnet, tapping the screwdriver on the engine block very lightly with the sledge.

WADE Anyway, truth is, you don't find this guy. He finds you. It's all Russian Mafia. Best I can do is point you in the direction of his competition.

Wade stands, and takes a giant swing at the engine block with the sledgehammer. The engine roars into life.

BOND Who's the competition?

Wade wipes his hands on a rag, gets ready to lower the bonnet.

WADE Ex-KGB guy, tough mother, got a bad limp on his right leg. Name's Zukovsky.

BOND Valentin Dimitreveych Zukovsky?

Wade slams the bonnet shut.

WADE Yeah. You know him?

BOND I gave him the limp.

DRESSED TO KILL

LINDY HEMMING: COSTUME DESIGNER

THE JAMES BOND LOOK

NAME Pierce Brosnan
BORN 16 May 1953
JOB Actor

HEIGHT 6ft 1in CHEST 42 in WAIST 32/33in
INSIDE LEG 34 in SHOE SIZE 11–11 ½

SUITS Designer, Lindy Hemming
Manufacturer: Brioni, Italy
1. Grey suit with box cover check, worn with waistcoat
2. Blue blazer, gold buttons
3. Prince of Wales check suit
4. Cream lightweight suit, with a biscuit dot in fabric
5. Dinner suit, with waistcoat
6. Navy birdseye blue suit, three buttoned,
long-bodied, single-breasted

All the following from Sulka, New York and
Bond Street, London
SHIRTS Three: Sky blue; ivory and white linen.
TIES Woven silk, classic ties, in mostly blue with
yellow and red
HANDKERCHIEFS Dark blue handkerchief in
breast pocket; white with evening suit.
SWEATER Cashmere, cable knit, with crew neck
when driving sports car, off duty in Monte Carlo
DRESS SHIRTS White with pleated front
BOW TIES Self-tying black, in silk

SHOES Church, hand-made, English, long and narrow
1. Black, between a brogue and toe-cap
2. Brown brogues
3. Evening shoes
4. Timberland boots, from Timberland, for all action
   wear

Lindy Hemming refused to begin designing anything for Pierce Brosnan until they had had a series of meetings: 'He is establishing his own look as Bond – I wanted him to be constantly consulted,' she says.

'We wanted him to look modern, but not trendy like someone in advertising. Although he should have a tailored look, brought up on the Savile Row tradition, his lifestyle has changed.

'Here is someone who works in air-conditioned buildings and jumps on planes to travel to key locations. Pierce's own demands were that the designs had to reflect the lightness of modern man, but still be svelte and smooth.'

Lindy, who counts last year's big British hit *Four Weddings and a Funeral* among her past movies, then began a search to find a manufacturer to match her designs and expectations.

She finally opted for Brioni of Italy, which usually pitch their low-profile business at royalty, leading politicians and millionaires, who pay around £4,000 a suit.

'I went to visit their factory on the Adriatic, where they were in the middle of an order from the King of Malaysia who wanted a whole range of clothes for a big family wedding,' she says.

'They have eighteen master tailors, eighteen second-class tailors, ten women who do button holes only, ten who do lining canvasses and ten who specialise in trousers. I have never seen anything like it, outside Hong Kong.'

But even Brioni was slightly taken aback by the size of the order: Pierce would need between twelve and seventeen of each suit, all identical in every detail.

For many scenes Pierce is wearing one, a stunt man another and a walk-on double third. Also, the second unit is often in action with stunt men only, delivering the sort of high-speed danger which no actor could risk.

'On top of this, we have to hold back spares to replace damaged clothes and brand new suits in case Pierce has to re-shoot earlier scenes,' says Lindy. 'It all arrived immaculately. The insides are light, the material soft and everything looks tailor-made.'

Lindy Hemming gives her inside secrets on some of the key designs and reasons behind the clothes on *GoldenEye* …

French Connection. Again, as with all the main characters, there are several outfits. She also has a tapestry coat from Kenko, with Afghan lamb collar, cuffs and hem, which cost well over £1,000. Her sexier clothes consist of a silk slip dress, which I designed, with a fabric by Christian Le Croix, a sarong from Ghost and bikini from La Pearla which is my homage to Ursula Andress.'

XENIA (FAMKE JANSSEN)

'She has eight main outfits, mostly black, but which include a grey suit in the style of Thierry Mugler which she wears for important scenes in Monte Carlo. Her hats are designed by Phillip Sommerville, who is hat-maker to the Royal Family. Jimmy Choo, who designs and makes shoes for Princess Diana, provided all her shoes.'

TREVELYAN (SEAN BEAN)

'He is a man of mystery, so we put him in black for most of the time, to be sleek and menacing. The highlight of his wardrobe is a leather overcoat with mink collar, worn over a grey cashmere polo-neck, from Mulberry. It cost well over £2,000. In the train sequence, he's in a slim-tailored, high-fastening double-breasted black suit, the slate grey shirt from Donna Karan and Armani tie.'

NATALYA (IZABELLA SCORUPCO)

'She has modern clothing, most of which is bought. Kurt Geiger lace-up boots, opaque tights, a box-pleated swing mini-skirt from Joseph, a floppy crepe embroidered skirt by Ghost and a short cardigan from

rather cruel and vulgar in taste, with lots of jewellery. Robbie was a little taken aback, actually.'

BORIS (ALAN CUMMING)

'I went through *Wired* magazine, which is a speciality publication for computer and Internet fanatics, to pick up ideas. Boris lives for his computer wizardry, so I put him in a *Wired* T-shirt for one scene, with long, baggy shorts. He never thinks of what he's wearing and had to look as if he didn't care.'

CAROLINE (SERENA GORDON)

'I dressed her like a Sloane: white shirt, jacket, scarf, dark stockings, short skirt and pearl earrings. The suit was by Pied-à-Terre. It was meant to be so you would think she is a serious girl. But when she kisses Bond, she falls apart.'

M (JUDI DENCH)

'She had to be stylish and sharp and powerful. I put her in a Sonja Rykiel suit. It is a cream, heavy crepe, with pewter buttons and a Mandarin collar, worn with dark brown sheer tights and chocolate brown shoes from Joanna & David.'

MISS MONEYPENNY (SAMANTHA BOND)

'We wanted a far more sophisticated, up-market look, since she is going out for the evening in her scene with Bond. I designed a black dress, with a crepe Empire-line body, a very low boat neckline and tight black sleeves. Both Moneypenny and M's outfits had to contrast with offices designed in tan, chrome and beige.'

VALENTIN (ROBBIE COLTRANE)

'Mr Eddy in Berwick Street, Soho, London always makes Robbie's suits. But I added to my designs with a waistcoat of small pheasant feathers, made by Favourbrook of Piccadilly Arcade, London. I wanted the look of a big Russian man who goes hunting and is

IRINA (MINNIE DRIVER)

'I had some fun with this one. I went for an over-the-top Marilyn Monroe look, with a red satin dress that had black, embroidered flowers on it, with lots of cleavage. Her backing group wears skating skirts, fishnet tights and white cowboy boots, with wide belts, stetsons and holsters. You go mad once in a while with Bond designs – and that was my moment.'

Pierce Brosnan's Bond never had a close shave throughout filming. Make-up supervisor Linda DeVetta insisted that he kept some stubble to 'rough you up a bit'.

The make-up crew gather around Izabella
on set, to repair the ravages of filming.

LINDA DEVETTA:
MAKE-UP SUPERVISOR

Whatever the mood and whatever the hour, the first person that Pierce Brosnan meets at the studio or location each morning is Linda DeVetta. As Make-Up Supervisor, she is also never far from his side for the remainder of the day.

But when they met at his rented home in Hampstead, London two weeks before filming began, she delivered a shock: 'I am going to have to make you look a bit more rough and coarse.' she told him. 'In one respect, your features are a little too perfect.'

Linda, named by Oscar-winner Jeremy Irons and Sigourney Weaver as their personal favourite, explains: 'He is such a good-looking guy, I decided to leave a beard shadow in the whole time. He would look too smooth and too young without it.

'It means that he does not shave each morning. I shave him with clippers, instead, not taking it down to the skin. I don't do anything around the eyes, because I don't want to make him any more glamorous than he is already.

'I put on a foundation, which gives him a tan. He has a very pale Celtic complexion, and the Bond image is of a slightly tanned outdoor action man.

'I am glad to say that he has five freckles on his nose and I try to leave those in, because his face needs as many imperfections as possible. I just soften them slightly.'

Linda, who also has Jane Royale and Trefor Proud on her make-up team, delivers her make-up secrets on some of the main cast:

IZABELLA SCORUPCO (Natalya): 'The simplest make-up, because she is such a beauty. A little work on the eyes, just mascara and hardly any definition. There is nothing you'd want to change in her features.'

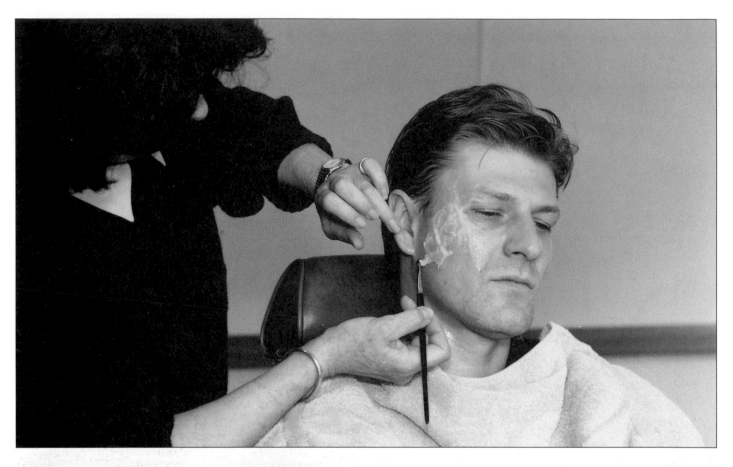

SEAN BEAN (Trevelyan): 'Because his character has a burn on the side of his face, Sean's in the make-up chair for an hour. I use Dermplast, a Swiss-made prosthetic developed over ten years by two chemists and a make-up artist. The stuff has to be melted in a microwave, then poured in to the cast and it goes into the fridge to set. I use five small pieces to build the scar on Sean's face every morning.'

JUDI DENCH (M): 'She has the most beautiful face, but as she is sixty my brief is to make her look as young and glamorous as possible. I use foundation to make her lovely blue eyes shine out. She is blonde and fair, but can take a lot of definition.'

ALAN CUMMING (Boris): 'The character sits in front of a computer all day, so is scruffy and dishevelled. I make him very pale and paint blue shadow on his eyes. He is bloodless and never sees the light of day. He never shaved, so I just used clippers on him each morning.'

SAMANTHA BOND (Moneypenny): 'She is not an easy face to make up. It was difficult to find the Moneypenny look without it seeming old hat, because these films have been going on since the Sixties and you are trying to re-invent a look, while keeping the essence of the original. We went for sophistication this time.'

FAMKE JANSSEN (Xenia): 'A much more difficult face, because her features are very strong. Famke is also playing a baddie. I put foundation on her which is much lighter than her natural colour. She is a Dutch girl with a Latin look and olive skin, despite the fact she never goes near the sun. Her natural colour does not suit her and she looks prettier with a paler skin. I work under

Tiger pilot: The biggest challenge for the make-up department was to turn the male pilot of the Tiger helicopter into a double for Xenia (Famke Janssen). He had a beard stubble and a pony-tail. He was given a brunette wig and hour-long make-over so audiences will believe that glamorous Famke is indeed at the controls.

the eyes with a concealer, then curl her eyelashes and eyebrows up. Her eyebrows are plucked but they are a perfect shape – very dark and very thin. I brush them out and set them with hair lacquer to make them slightly softer.'

They said it could never happen: James
Bond in Russia. Jeeps are being retrieved
from a canal in St Petersburg during the
hugely ambitious tank-chase sequence.

TO RUSSIA, WITH LOVE

BARBARA BROCCOLI: Producer

It was going to be Pierce Brosnan's most unusual test. He was going to be the first James Bond to cross the border into Russia itself and work behind what were traditional lines of cold war and deep suspicion.

But the plan did not quite work out. Brosnan stayed at home along with the first unit, while the second unit visited for just eleven days of key sequences.

Producer Barbara Broccoli was left to take charge in St Petersburg and answer the questions from a Russian press, enjoying a new-found freedom, about why there had been changes in plan.

Says Barbara: 'As we began preparation within Russia, we started to realise there was a lot of red tape to cut through. It is not their fault, but we are used to working in cities which are familiar with filming schedules and methods.

'We also had an extra complication. We felt that if we were driving 36-ton tanks around the streets for four weeks we would out-stay our welcome.

'There was the weight of the tanks going over certain streets and we started to be concerned about damage, to gas pipes and water mains and such like. The question of liability was complicated: how fragile were these pipes and mains in the first place?

'The bills to put them right could have been enormous. The risk was too great. And there was also a lot of uncertainty in Russia at the time. We had to come to terms with the fact that perhaps our expectations and ambition had become too great.'

Breaking barriers between cultures. The jeeps nose-dive into the water in St Petersburg.

This is where Barbara's experience came into play. She has grown up with Bond, being only a baby when father Cubby was co-producing the debut movie *Dr No*, and there has been no easy ticket to the top job. With a budget of tens of millions dollars and knowing that a huge box office gross is required just to break even, there is no place for family sentiment.

Barbara was an assistant director on *Octopussy* and *A View To A Kill* and became associate producer for the last two 007 films, *The Living Daylights* and *Licence To Kill*.

Reports Barbara: 'The visit to Russia proved one thing for certain: our script is accurate. There seemed to be a real mafia arms-dealing presence and we visited a large market where they openly sell weapons, which inspired our scene with Valentin.

'You also find that in certain restaurants there are guys walking around with Italian suits and bad haircuts and Mercedes and BMWs parked outside.

'It is clear from reports that there is a huge problem of arms. Of course Bond operates in a world of heightened reality but it was uncanny how right the feeling was.'

There were also some welcoming aspects: 'St Petersburg is one of the most beautiful cities in the world and more European than Moscow or the rest of Russia,'

go ahead, is particularly exciting.'

On *GoldenEye*, confidence is high. But Barbara adds a realistic note: 'Although I have fallen in love with this movie, until the film is shown to an audience, you never know.

'It is like bringing home a boyfriend you love and introducing him to your parents. Every woman knows what I mean.'

PETER LAMONT: Production Designer

Peter Lamont's task was stark and simple: He had to build a section of the Russian city of St Petersburg along the disused runway of Leavesden Airfield, near Watford.

The new message came when all plans seemed to be set. The film's first unit, with Bond actor Pierce Brosnan, was to be in St Petersburg for a least a week. The second unit, filming action scenes of an amazing tank chase, would be there for three weeks.

Then the Russians became nervous about what had been agreed. Yes, a thirty-six-ton tank could still use some of their streets. But if any sewer, gas main, electricity cable or cobblestone was damaged, the film company must pay in full to a limit to be decided by the local authorities.

'It was an impossible demand,' says Peter. 'We would have no idea of what was already in need of repair, and the costs could have run into millions of dollars.

'We had already asked to film in one particular place and the Russians had quoted $15 million. In other words, no thanks – unless you're mad enough to pay.

So Peter and his design team got to work, with an increase in budget from MGM of a further half a million dollars. But savings were made by cancelling first unit filming in St Petersburg, and the second unit trimmed back to little more than a week.

'From the first piece of tubular scaffolding that went up to the first filming was just six weeks and four days.' he says proudly. 'It was a heck of a feat and just shows what can be done, when we're really up against it.'

> **'Destruction' of St Petersburg:** Some of the false destruction of St Petersburg by the second unit crew was too realistic for local authorities. The wife of the Mayor of St Petersburg was horrified when she saw them tearing down what she thought were beautiful balustrades in the city. She called her husband, who ordered out the militia. Filming was halted and the crew were booked on flights home the next day. Finally, amid much confusion, at three o'clock in the morning, Art Director Andrew Ackland-Snow was able to prove that the balustrades were no more than timber, made and constructed by the film crew itself. They were given a reprieve.

she says. 'The people are very special and love their city, with great reason.

'The local crew we worked with were extraordinary and obtained for us every pass that was going. However, we were certainly aware that the city, like Russia as a whole, is in enormous conflict.

'Whenever there are economic problems, certain people will always exploit the situation and that is exactly what is happening. Capitalism is a new force. It is a testing ground and new frontier.

'Besides, the attitude that my father has had in thirty-five years of making these movies is that we should always leave a place as we found it, if not better. It should be happy to have another film company come in. He believes in being careful and responsible – and so do we.

'Throughout it all, we also had the comfort of knowing we could set up a situation at Leavesden, linking with the film footage we took in Russia, which would look superb.'

And on the success of Bond itself. Barbara agrees: 'It is extraordinary. Eon has a long relationship with the British film industry, in Cubby's case since 1952.

'The idea that we could have now started off what just might be another film studio at Leavesden, if plans

It was the biggest change in plans during the making of GOLDENEYE.

The complex filming sequences on the streets of St Petersburg proved too impractical and, potentially, too costly for the first unit. So Production Designer Peter Lamont was asked to bring St Petersburg to Leavesden. With a budget

increase of half a million
dollars he designed a set
to match the real thing.
Extensive building work
went ahead on the disused
runway at Leavesden and
was completed in six
weeks and four days. The
final result even fooled
Film Editor Terry
Rawlings: 'I defy anyone to
tell the difference on
screen,' he says.

The tank does its worst. One of the many reasons why filming the entire sequence in St Petersburg was judged to be a veritable minefield of potential problems.

The vast structure, made up of more than 62 miles of scaffolding, finished at 750 feet long, 50 feet wide and 45 feet high. It included the original alleyway, bridge, roundabout and military vehicle park which were always earmarked for building at Leavesden – because they had to be destroyed in the tank chase.

'The street is a composite of several, rather than one in particular,' says Peter. 'But once filming started on it, I defy anyone to tell that we aren't in the heart of the city itself.'

There were other advantages. The tank, given a strict 15mph speed limit in St Petersburg, was able to get up to speeds of 45mph on the film set.

As Production Designer, it was Peter's job to produce stunning and original sets. But before he did so, he made pre-production visits to St Petersburg, Monte Carlo and Puerto Rico.

It was in Puerto Rico that he saw the world's largest spherical radio telescope at Arecibo. That becomes the headquarters for the Janus Syndicate.

This is Peter's fifteenth consecutive Bond. He began his remarkable winning streak in 1964 on *Goldfinger* as a draughtsman in the art department. But he is unwilling to

Derek Meddings, Miniature Effects Supervisor, with one of his most taxing challenges, turning a corner of Leavesden into the Siberian Arctic.

compare the five actors who have played 007 since then.

'I never allow myself to think about the man who plays James Bond,' he says. 'My job is to give them sets to work in which will surprise and amaze a cinema audience.

'In this, I'm particularly pleased with the settings for the Cuban control centre. There are also nice new angles to well-known sets: M's office and Q's workshop are nothing like we have ever seen on a Bond film.

He also delivered a cost-cutting plan to avoid shooting in Norway or Iceland for mountain scenes, having watched yet again the visually stunning 1946 film *Black Narcissus*, set in the Himalayas.

'In reality, they never left Pinewood Studios,' he says. 'I thought: "If they were doing that sort of work then, what can we achieve now?" So we have created our own mountain range on one of the sound stages here which looks terrific.'

Peter's last film before joining Bond was *True Lies*, the highly-acclaimed action thriller with Arnold Schwarzenegger which was compared with 007 by many critics.

But he says loyally: '*True Lies* was never Bond and never talked about like that when it was being made. The main character had a wife bored out of her skull and an out-of-control daughter. That was not James Bond.'

THE GREAT SPECTACULAR

The tank chase

Not for the first time on Bond, the key words were: 'It has not been tried before.'

This one was a tank chase. Very fast. In St Petersburg, Russia. With a dozen Lada police cars wrecked. Others crushed. Buildings shattered. Oh, and by the way, a statue of Tsar Nicholas sitting on a winged horse has to disintegrate – leaving the horse astride the tank's turret.

The complex action sequence, in which Bond gives chase in a tank behind General Ourumov (Gottfried John) and his hostage Natalya (Izabella Scorupco) across St Petersburg, is one of the most amazing of any 007 movie.

But, first: get the tank.

Three Russian tanks were purchased, costing between £9,000 and £14,000 each. Two were T54s (which means simply they were built in 1954) and the other a T55. They were heavy, cumbersome, old fashioned. All three would be used at some point, though obviously they were supposed to represent one tank.

Then Special Effects Supervisor Chris Corbould got to work with the team: 'We had to make them look more vicious, modern – and identical,' he says. 'They came with steel tracks, which tear up tarmac and streets. So we bought some rubber tracks from Chieftain tanks and changed all the sprockets to use them.

'Even what looks the most obvious thing in the script needs to be tested. The tank going over cars seemed straightforward, but once we drove it over various cars from breaker's yards, it seemed that it would never repeat

the same action twice.

'In the end, cars were being sent in from the breaker's yard by the ton – and the price was going up. But we did get a system of how they could be destroyed and know what was to happen.'

One of the biggest problems was getting the statue on top of the tank. Many technical methods were considered, but they went ahead with a simple solution.

'The tank had to drive along at 35 miles an hour, hit the bottom of the plinth and scoop up the statue on top,' says Chris. 'We put up the model of a horse, with the Tsar on top, and made a loop underneath the statue which we felt might just catch.

'We thought of complex and complicated methods, but I thought: 'This one is worth a go.' As it happened, we drove the tank at it and the statue stuck – first take. We could not believe it.'

Sequences like that need some good fortune. All the technical drawings, sketches and theories mean nothing without a slice of luck.

It was also needed in plenty on shooting, according to second unit director Ian Sharp: 'Everything we did with the tanks was dangerous,' he says. 'A tank is 38 tons of metal moving at speed and they cannot stop quickly.

'A lot of Russian vehicles we used are not good and there is a danger of them stalling, with a stunt man stranded in the car. We almost had a tank crashing into a Lada in Russia through a stall, and the luck factor helped us out.'

Stunt man Gary Powell was the tank's driver in the high-speed chases. He had to learn from scratch, but was soon manoeuvring the hefty vehicle with dexterity.

'We can genuinely get up to 45mph with the adapted tanks, if there's a good run-up,' says Ian. 'I have also made it look faster.

'We normally film at twenty-four frames a second, so I have slowed the frame speed down to eighteen or sixteen. The moment you get below the twenty-four frames the actors in the picture have to move very slowly to balance it, otherwise it will look like an old black and white silent movie.'

But it was with some relief that Ian, who was also Second Unit Director on *Who Framed Roger Rabbit?* and was Launch Director on the successful TV series *Robin of Sherwood*, received the news that the planned St Petersburg set was to be extended.

'For what we wanted to achieve, being on location in St Petersburg itself would have been a nightmare,' he says. 'Instead, we went there for eight days shooting and achieved some great results.

'On one Sunday morning, we had a tank turning 360 degrees outside the Astoria Hotel, which is the equivalent of the Dorchester or Ritz in London. We also did the same thing outside a cathedral.

'There were sixty crew and 200 Russian technicians and it was all very well organised. But there were obvious restrictions, which would probably have become worse as filming went on.'

Even back at Leavesden there were some mishaps: 'On one day we lost the camera crew. My cameraman had a steel splinter in his eye, picked up from one of the rigs. Then the Land Rover tracking vehicle turned over on one of the corners and we lost the focus puller and loader, who were both taken to hospital for checks.'

Perrier and the tank: Perrier supplied a total of 90,000 tins for a collision scene between a lorry and the tank on the St Petersburg set. But most of the cans were empty – because they could cause a dangerous explosion on impact. Bond bosses then received a request that all the empty cans be totally destroyed by the tank itself. The reason? Perrier did not want to risk them being misused and re-filled by rival drink manufacturers.

The dish in Arecibo, Puerto Rico
- doubling for the Cuban control centre in
GOLDENEYE - had to be matched perfectly
at Leavesden, to a scale of one-twentieth.

Bond in miniature

Two MiG 29 jet fighters took off in formation above Leavesden Airfield and clipped each other's wings. Had they been real, it could have resulted in a fireball which might have engulfed the whole place. But these MiGs were only nine feet long and expertly controlled from the ground by radio.

Miniature Effects Supervisor Derek Meddings will be defying audiences to tell the difference between what is real, full-sized and actual to the work by his team of model makers.

He started in August 1994 preparing for vital scenes. The MiGs were the first. They were exactly one-seventh of the real size, and made to scaled-down detail.

They used ducted fans inside, developed to ten horsepower, and three specialists controlled them. Speed on take-off was around 60mph and they flew at 90mph for crash scenes at Severnaya.

Derek, an experienced operator on his sixth Bond movie, surrounded himself with familiar faces. He originally worked with Brian Smithies, chief model maker, on *Thunderbirds* and teamed up with cameraman Paul Wilson on *Superman The Movie*. *Superman* won Derek an Oscar; he also received an Oscar nomination for the 007 film, *Moonraker*.

But the team needed all their skill for the Cuban control headquarters and giant dish which is submerged beneath a lake. A small reservoir was set up next to the dish, so water could be piped in and out.

'The dish is made of concrete and to control the water and flooding was very difficult,' said Derek. 'But it was a huge advantage being at Leavesden. We had all the space we needed and the privacy to do things our own way.'

A model train was constructed to match Trevelyan's special train, adapted to look aggressive and threatening, at Nene Valley Railway, near Peterborough.

The restored station, used for tourists and steam enthusiasts, is seen as a semi-derelict Soviet military rail depot. Trevelyan's train crashes into the Russian tank, manned by Bond.

'We built just one model train and crashed it twice on tracks we built at Leavesden,' reports Derek. 'The tank is made out of fibreglass, and we also added an explosion at the point of contact. The film footage from the real train was then matched perfectly with what we had filmed.'

The bungee jump

It was a drop of 640 feet next to a wall of concrete. It looks dangerous, it is dangerous and proves to be the most spectacular opening shot of any Bond film as 007 swallow-dives at 100mph towards the ground.

Stunt Co-ordinator Simon Crane had calculated the dive to the second, to the inch and to the pound. The bungee cord was made of separate threads which would give four clear seconds of free fall before engaging.

Stuntman Wayne Michaels was set to make the jump, from the top of a dam near Locarno, Switzerland, and four cameras were on him from every angle.

'We work non-stop to make stunts absolutely safe for the excitement of the cinema audience,' says Simon,

Dropping in: The Oxford University bungee jump team was consulted in planning the spectacular 600-foot-plus plunge along the side of a dam near Locarno, Switzerland, which opens *GoldenEye*. Their advice: 'It's never been done so close to a sheer wall of concrete. You're jumping into the unknown.'

who set a record himself for the world's first jet-to-jet mid-air transfer in Sylvester Stallone's thriller, *Cliffhanger*. 'But at that moment of truth, on a jump that has never been attempted before, you always wonder …'

The sequence shows Bond falling, pulling out a gun and firing a piton into the top of a concrete building. He then hauls himself down and into a Soviet nerve gas centre to attempt to destroy it.

The jump was executed perfectly – then had to be done again, with a shorter 250-foot drop, to show the gun being lined up for shooting.

Simon, who has himself doubled for ex-Bond Timothy Dalton in *Licence To Kill*, Mel Gibson in *Air*

America and Kevin Costner in *Robin Hood: Prince of Thieves*, says: 'If you thought of the risks when making the jump, then you'd never do it.'

Because of the proximity of the sheer concrete wall of the dam, the bungee cord was connected to a crane which the audience will not see.

Special effects expert Nick Finlayson was watching the drop from the roof of the building, since he had rigged a piton to fire separately with explosive force. The piton gun was designed around the Sparklet Soda Siphon carbon dioxide charge during six weeks of experimentation.

'The jump was an incredible sight,' reports Nick. 'Frightening and exciting at the same moment, but also very graceful. Wayne was bruised on his back and legs – and never said a word.'

Chris Corbould: Special Effects Supervisor

Chris Corbould began work on *GoldenEye* a full eight months before the first scene was filmed at Leavesden Airfield. While actors were attending auditions, he was already working out the details of what were to be his greatest problems.

'The script was still being re-drafted, so some of the work had to be changed,' he says. 'For example, we built a full-sized MiG 21 plane, which we were going to send down a wire and crash into a building. It was then switched to a MiG 29, and it was not to be crashed in the same way.

'But those sort of things happen constantly on big-budget Bond movies, when ideas are being improved all

Filming inch-perfect models of MiG fighters against a blue background in one of the sound stages gives an opportunity to add precise visual effects to the sequence in the editing stage.

the time. You're always trying to aim for the spectacular – things that have never been seen or done before.

'The result is that we make so many prototypes, working objects which are brand new one-offs. I hired a special effects crew of about forty, and it was constantly involved in a mixture of invention, heavy duty work and high-quality engineering skills.'

This is the seventh Bond for Chris, but his first as Special Effects Supervisor. There is a strict structure in the film industry, which demands that all Special Effects Technicians must have at least ten years' experience before they become Senior Technicians. Then they must serve a further five years before even being considered for the top job.

Chris lists his problems and solutions for the seven greatest challenges for 007.

001

PROBLEM   A Pilatus Porter plane was needed in the opening sequence to appear to be about to take off. But no plane could be found to guarantee a ground speed steady and constant enough for the safety of the crew and stunt doubles.

SOLUTION   The Art department bought us an old plane of this type, which had crashed, and we re-built it. We put in an Alfa Romeo car engine and drive axles to the wheel of the plane, linking a rotor blade of our own into the engine. We got it up to a rock-solid 40mph for fight sequences.

002

PROBLEM Our first big sequence of explosions came in Severnaya station. We had a 30-foot-high radardish coming down dangerously close to the actors.

SOLUTION   We worked out a system of hydraulically telescoping it down, and weaved it among the rafters.

Bond and Trevelyan fight it out, lying flat towards the left of this picture in a sea of green. Dramatic details are added by digital computer on to a 'green screen' at the editing stage of their final encounter.

003

PROBLEM The antenna on the vast dish in Arecibo, Puerto Rico (in the film it is Cuba), has to be used in close-up for the big fight sequence between Bond and Trevelyan. We had to match the long-distance shots taken on location.

SOLUTION We made six different sections of the antenna, in steel, ranging down from 90 feet in length. We filmed against three different backgrounds: a false sky backing; a green screen (with the background added digitally later) and outside against a real sky, with the camera on a helicopter whizzing around it.

Problem 006: During Bond's attack on the Nerve Gas Centre in the opening sequence, the barrels did not at first shoot forward dramatically enough. They were finally propelled from a customised conveyor belt, to make them look far more spectacular.

004

PROBLEM A big shoot-out in the Archives between Bond and Russian soldiers, and the sheer fire power demanded. The exploding bullets have to be planted individually.

SOLUTION We worked into the night to plant a total of 1,800 bullet hits, all specially wired. I don't think there has been more in any scene in any film.

005

PROBLEM Getting liquid nitrogen to look real as Boris (Alan Cumming) is frozen. We tested twelve different methods, ranging from real liquid nitrogen over dummies – which did not work too well – to carbon dioxide and just white dust.

SOLUTION We used water in a 300-gallon tank, being instantly poured from a huge chute on to fifty blocks of dry ice. The effect over Alan Cumming was terrific.

006

PROBLEM In the Nerve Gas Plant, Bond shoots the lock from a storage pen and there are 160 barrels in sixteen rows which are supposed to shoot forward. Every one plopped pathetically down rather than springing forward.

SOLUTION We had to make every rank up individually with a pneumatically-operated conveyor belt which threw these barrels off. The barrels were then made of lightweight foam so we could get stunt men underneath to take the fall.

007

PROBLEM The size of explosions in the headquarters of the Janus Syndicate, the Cuban control centre at the end of the film. Director Martin Campbell wanted one big shot of everything blowing to pieces, with eight separate cameras.

SOLUTION We tested for close on one month, with thirty-five different explosions, every day to get the timing perfect. We had individual explosions making up one blast. It was for a four-second sequence.

GUNS, BOATS, PLANES, CARS AND GADGETS

GUNS: Charlie Bodycomb

Armourer Charlie Bodycomb was always at hand whenever Pierce Brosnan fired Bond's famous gun, the Walther PPK, 7.65mm. The real thing was used in close-up, firing blanks, because Bodycomb feared that some gun experts in cinema audiences would spot if it was a replica.

'The basic design hasn't changed much since it was first introduced for German officers and police forces in 1931,' he says. 'It is a weapon, with seven rounds, which will kill at close range.

'They are manufactured in a factory at Ulm-am-Donau and there has always been a regular demand, even before Bond named it as his personal favourite. It fits the Bond image because of its smooth lines and excellent handling.

'Ironically, it is still issued by the British Army to undercover personnel operating in plain clothes, because

it is neat and easily disguised.'

The Walther PPK 7.65mm is just over 6 inches in length, and weighs about 1¼ lbs.

Charlie was also taking no chances with his supply of thirty Kalashnikov AKS74 rifles for use by the extras – some of them trained soldiers – who were playing Russians during filming.

He carefully checked and counted each one in and out, every time they were in use. The extras had to show a clean barrel and put the gun's magazine, with blanks, into a separate pile. All the numbers of the guns were then double-checked.

'The safety aspect is always most important when guns are being used,' says Charlie. 'Then comes the security of knowing that each one is being returned. They were difficult to get.

'The magazines, for example, were captured from the PLO by the Israelis on the West Bank. Only Soviet weapons have these distinctive orange plastic pistol grips and magazines.'

The gun itself, with a thirty-shot detachable box, fires 800 rounds a minute and is manufactured in Tula, Russia, Poland and China.

'I am afraid that the part of the script which deals with gun-running in the new-style Russia is chillingly accurate,' says Charlie. 'Even as a gun dealer, you cannot officially buy them. Each one was obtained through long-standing contacts.

The other guns on display, in the key scene between Bond and gun dealer Valentin, (Robbie Coltrane), are the Heckler and Koch MP5 sub-machine gun and the Glock 17.

'The Heckler and Koch is German, now made under licence in the UK,' says Charlie. 'It has thirty rounds and is the gun carried by police at Heathrow Airport.

'The Glock 17 is made in Austria and they've had great success selling to the American police. That is the one that Valentin admires.'

The Manticore

Moored in Monte Carlo – where Bond discovers the body of Admiral Farrell and realises that Xenia is using a decoy 'Admiral' to help her steal a Tiger helicopter from *La Fayette* warship – the *Manticore*'s real name is *Northern Cross*. It is a $15 million yacht, the property of Finnish businessman Jorma Lillbacka, who owns the power machine company, Finn-Power.

The yacht is normally moored in Antibes in the South of France and is chartered in the summer for $400,000 a month. It sleeps twelve and has a crew of eight.

Top speed: 28 knots. Range: 2,500 nautical miles at 15 knots. Inside, it is covered with Lapland birch, which has thirty-two coats of varnish. There are six bedrooms and a bar, saloon dining area and three sun decks. It is 144 feet long and 45 feet above the waterline.

La Fayette

Bond runs on to the ship to try and prevent Xenia from flying off in the Tiger helicopter before an unsuspecting ship's crew and a party of guests. He is stopped by guards.

La Fayette is a new French-built stealth ship, one of only six launched so far. It looks more like a vast model ship than the real thing, with no portholes and a mixture of dark grey, dove grey and dolphin grey colours. One of its unique selling points is that if it is hit by a shell, the shell passes straight through without exploding.

It is manned by twelve officers, sixty-eight petty officers and sixty-one ratings and seamen with a helicopter detachment of twelve. It has a top speed of 25 knots and a range of 7,000 miles at 15 knots average speed.

Firing power includes eight Exocet 40 missiles, one short-range surface to air Crotale system and one 100mm gun with CADAM new-type mount.

The stolen Tiger. The £10 million helicopter is snatched by Xenia from a NATO frigate moored in Monte Carlo.

The new BMW Roadster Z3 turned heads whenever it was filmed, since the car was being used by Bond many months in advance of its official launch.

Tiger helicopter

This is the top secret and valuable (£10 million each) helicopter, which Bond is trying to save from falling into the hands of Xenia and the Janus Syndicate.

It is an Anglo Franco-German Eurocopter, set to go into service in the year 2003. The selling points are agility, night combat and air-to-air combat.

The fly-by-night system allows the pilot to put on a visor, through which he can see all features ahead of him in various shades of green. It also gives him speed and height on the screen, in virtual reality style, so he can control the helicopter at high speeds.

The pilot is in charge of the four air-to-air missiles; the chief navigator is responsible for eight anti-tank missiles.

The top speed is 170 knots – which is 180mph – and it can loop the loop at 120 knots, a unique feature which is used in *GoldenEye*, with Xenia executing a victory roll after Bond's vain efforts to stop her skyjacking the supersecret stealth craft from the deck of a closely-guarded NATO frigate.

Cars

There are four main cars used in *GoldenEye*.

1964 Aston Martin DB5

The favourite. Powered from 0–60 in 8.1 seconds, and with a top speed of 148.2mph. Originally cost £4,175 and now worth between £30,000 and £50,000.

BMW Roadster

A brand new sports car yet to be launched, with all specifications as yet formally untested. 0–60 in 8.5 seconds. Top speed: 130mph. Price: approx $35,000.

Ferrari 355

Xenia's car. 0–60 in 4.7 seconds. Top speed: 186mph. Price $84,864.37.

Zabrosh (Moskvich)

A clapped-out Russian car model used by CIA agent Jack Wade (Joe Don Baker). Bond car expert Freddie Wilmington, who has been working on the vehicle,

How the other half lives. Bond commiserates with Jack Wade (Joe Don Baker) on his CIA 'company car' allocation.

gives the speeds as 0–60: Next month. Top speed: next year. Price: we'll pay you to take it away.

The repairs and maintenance of Russian cars were the responsibility of Freddie Wilmington, who runs Vision Vehicle Hire of Pinner, Middlesex, which specialises in providing vehicles of all ages for movies.

'I had three brand new Volga cars, costing a little over £9,000 each, to use in the tank chase,' he reports. 'There were only about forty kilometres on the clock of each of them, but I had to put on low profile tyres and new suspension to improve them. Even so, they are about thirty years behind the times and can never be used on a British road because they don't come up to our safety standards.'

There was also a total of fourteen Lada cars, used as police cars, all of which were destroyed in the chase scenes.

Q's gadgets

Nick Finlayson, Senior Special Effects expert, prepared Q's gadgets for three months before the filming sequences, which took just one and a half days.

'All could have gone wrong in the space of a few hours on the film set and my work – along with my reputation – would have been wasted,' he observes.

This was Nick's fourth Bond movie. He also did special effects work on films like *Aliens* and *Willow*. He gives his own guide to the working of gadgets we see in action in Q's workshop.

Rocket across the workshop: 'We put tungsten wire between the end of the wheelchair, which is mounted in a steel tube to take exhaust heat away from Desmond Llewellyn, who plays Q. We tie it off to a "safebox", a 3 feet square wooden cube, with a metal plate at the back of it. The rocket smacks against the metal plate and comes to a dead stop, across forty feet, taking half a second to travel the distance. When the rocket travels along the wire, it sometimes breaks the wire, so that is why there is a safebox. It is a standard German flare rocket.'

Wheelchair: 'It is a German-made Chetah G24S-PRO from Beard Brothers, Oxford which cost £7,500. It is a motorised, Class 3 vehicle, registered for the road and off-road use too, with electric tilt seats and leg-rests. There is even a Recaro racing seat. We built two buttons into the left-hand console. One was a dummy button. Desmond presses it and we ignited the rocket separately. With the other, Desmond could push it at any time and the cast splits and swings open to the left.'

Leather belt: 'The leather belt fires a rappelling line. At the end of that line is a piton, which is an armoured nail of about 1½ inches. The one fired from the belt is only about 8 feet, rather than the 75 feet of high tensile wire, because of practical considerations. There is a swift cut-away on camera and audiences see a larger piton hit the ceiling in close-up. Bond is seen to swing across in the next shot. The piton striking the ceiling is achieved by pulling it down a wire in the following shot. It is being pulled by dropping a weight on a system of pulleys. We use nylon low-tangle braid, which handles better. Bond is actually swinging on a piece of steel cable, for safety's sake. It is achieved on camera in a sequence of separate shots.'

Pen: 'It is a Parker stainless steel ball-point pen, costing £6.95. Initially, a flashing light was needed, so I replaced

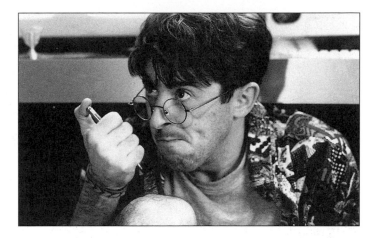

the ink cartridge with a flasher unit, driven by six miniature hearing aid batteries, less than 6mm in diameter, and we added a powerful LED (Light Emitting Diode). We did not need this in the end, because it was decided not to have a light on the pen. So it was back to using a plain pen. The two weeks' work it took to make was never needed. A pyrotechnic charge was placed into the mannequin and set off electrically. The mannequin disintegrated, because it was made of polyurethane foam.'

Bond Watch An Omega Seamaster Professional Diver Watch, made in Switzerland and selling at £895, is James Bond's choice of watch in *GoldenEye*. The 18ct gold version at £13,000 was rejected in favour of steel, since it is adapted to a laser beam in key sequences. Omega, founded in 1848, also supply watches to astronauts, including the first man on the moon, Neil Armstrong.

Martin Campbell: Director

Director Martin Campbell began each day at 4.30am. He would leave his wife, Carole and children Thomas, six, and Fabrice, eighteen months, sleeping at their rented house in Swiss Cottage, London, and be driven along dark, near-deserted roads for a 5.30am start at Leavesden.

For the following two hours, he would sit alone in his first floor office or walk the still-deserted sound stages and plan the day, fortified only by coffee. Then, at 7.30am, he took breakfast on the set itself and began filming at 8 o'clock sharp.

A transformation of the quietly-spoken, articulate New Zealand-born Campbell took place. For the next eleven hours, he became fast-moving and sharp-talking, with irritation occasionally boiling over to some harsh swearing, as he urged the crew and actors to work to the same high-energy level as him.

He never stopped talking, encouraging and joking until at least 7pm – even through the one-hour lunch he was often trouble-shooting – and the day was still not over. There was viewing of the 'rushes' with film editor Terry Rawlings for a further hour and selections to be made of the best take.

By the time Campbell had been taken home by his driver, there was time only for 'one very large glass of wine', a brief conversation with his wife and a look at his sleeping children before getting to bed by 10.30pm.

That was his system six days a week for twenty weeks – even on Sunday, he would work on administration from 10am to 5pm – and the cast often wondered how he kept going at such a slick pace.

'I don't know where my energy comes from,' says Campbell, who away from the film set seems to deflate and yawns through his few breaks. 'It works in that the cast and actors get swept up in the frenzy of it all and deliver the goods.'

But he did have fears about *GoldenEye*. They came before signing the contract and seeing the potential of the new script and the line-up of actors.

'I thought that Bond might be played out,' he admits. 'But I watched all sixteen Bond films on tape,just to remind myself what was good about them. The humour and action and romantic quality was there, to be developed and exploited in this seventeenth picture.

'I could see a way forward to make the leap into the Nineties and deliver a Bond just as classy, just as romantic, but hopefully even more unbeatable than the others.

'I also realised that we had nothing to worry about from the hype around the other action characters played by Bruce Willis, Arnold Schwarzenegger, Mel Gibson and Sylvester Stallone. These are blue-collar heroes and just do not have the sophistication or style of Bond.'

But Martin is disarmingly honest about his personal opinion of other Bond actors: 'Sean Connery was great and had the good fortune to be involved in the early films,which had particularly good narrative.

'Roger Moore was not my idea of Bond, but he did what he was best at, being self-effacing, light and he delivered some very good throw-away lines. Tim Dalton, I felt, looked too angry and unrelaxed.

'Once Pierce Brosnan was on board I felt that we could get on with delivering a great Bond movie. Pierce is absolutely right: the perfect 007. Born to play him, if you like, in the sense that he lights up the screen with a winning mixture of action, humour and romance. He's also a damned good actor and knows exactly what he's doing.'

This is Campbell's biggest movie by far. He directed the $20 million budget *No Escape*, but first established his reputation for directing episodes of popular British TV series like *The Professionals*, *Minder* and *Shoestring*.

In 1986, he directed the award-winning and most memorable *Edge of Darkness* drama series for the BBC, with Bob Peck and Joanne Whalley-Kilmer, and his name and reputation was fixed for the future.

'The size of the budget never worried me,' he insists. 'A film is a film and I do my best to deliver on time and to the highest standard.

'But you can't get away from the fact that it's a Bond movie. I became part of history, while remembering that I must not get carried away in the mists of time. I also did not allow myself to be side-tracked into thinking how much it was all costing.

'Instead, I concentrated on Pierce and saw him delivering performances of a lifetime as James Bond. I thought: "It's my job to capture that and make sure it's just as special and magical at the cinema." '

Terry Rawlings: Film Editor

Film Editor Terry Rawlings is regularly and anxiously asked by actors and backroom staff: 'Is the film going to be a winner?'

Terry is the only person on the film crew, apart from director Martin Campbell, to watch constantly the overall picture as he sits in his second floor editing rooms – usually listening to Vivaldi or jazz on his CD player – making sure that the best scenes and shots are used.

'Everyone concentrates on their own job, whether it's hair, make-up, costumes, special effects, lighting or acting,' he says. 'I see the results on a daily basis and have to work with them.

'Within a couple of weeks, I knew we had a terrific movie. Pierce Brosnan is the best James Bond since Sean Connery and the story is brilliant. Pierce is not only very handsome but he can be both dangerous and funny.

'The most important thing of all is that he has got vulnerability. He comes across as a human being, caught up in incredible situations.'

The results of the entire day's shooting, with its filming flaws and acting mistakes, are sent to laboratories at 8pm each evening. The jumbled finished product – called rushes in Britain and dailies in America – will be printed and delivered by 6.30am the following morning.

During the day, Rawlings and Campbell make their separate selections of what they think are the best takes and angles, whether they be close-up or long shot.

'We agree nine times out of ten on our selections,' says Terry, who counts *Alien*, *Alien³*, *Blade Runner* and *Chariots of Fire* among his films. 'But Martin always has the final word. I then put together the film, trying to keep up with changes and demands on a daily basis.'

Phil Meheux:
Director of photography

Phil Meheux shows Bond in an entirely new light. Audiences will notice an altogether darker, more forbidding atmosphere in *GoldenEye*. Meheux, who has photographed all Campbell's films since the 1987 movie, *Criminal Law*, was under strict instructions to make it what he calls "tough and dirty".

Pony-tailed Phil, whose career began in 1962 as a projectionist at Ealing Studios at the very point 007's debut in *Dr No* was winning world-wide recognition, plotted the lighting and angles for *GoldenEye*'s cameras.

Phil is a former BBC trainee who began operating the camera on outdoor sequences for the first TV police series, *Dixon Of Dock Green*, in the mid-sixties.

His credits include *Omen III - The Final Conflict*, *Who Dares Wins*, *The Honorary Consul*, *Max Headroom - The Original Story*, *The Fourth Protocol* and *Highlander II*.

Tom Pevsner:
Executive Producer

Tom Pevsner was the voice of experience when it came to keeping proper control of the lavish costs while making sure there would be a maximum effect on screen. His record and background has a stamp of sophistication, which he constantly brought to the job.

He served in the British Army and studied at Cambridge University before entering the film industry in 1951 under Sir Michael Balcon at Ealing Studios.

Tom's new lifestyle could have hardly been in sharper contrast to that of his father, the distinguished architectural historian, Sir Nikolaus Pevsner. He worked as first assistant director on Ealing classics like *The Ladykillers* and was later hired by a succession of celebrated movie-makers such as Billy Wilder, John Huston and John Ford.

He has been Associate Producer on Bond movies *For Your Eyes Only*, *Octopussy*, *A View To A Kill*, *The Living Daylights* and *Licence To Kill*.

Martin Campbell (far left) and Phil Meheux (far right) working together to give Bond a new look.